Cassandra Wilson-Bullock

dead christians walking

dead christians walking

CASSANDRA WILSON-BULLOCK

TATE PUBLISHING & *Enterprises*

Published by Tate Publishing & Enterprises, LLC
127 E. Trade Center Terrace | Mustang, Oklahoma 73064 USA
1.888.361.9473 | www.tatepublishing.com

Tate Publishing is committed to excellence in the publishing industry. The company reflects the philosophy established by the founders, based on Psalm 68:11,
"The Lord gave the word and great was the company of those who published it."

Book design copyright © 2010 by Tate Publishing, LLC. All rights reserved.
Cover design by Bekah Garibay
Interior design by Nathan Harmony

Published in the United States of America

ISBN: 978-1-61739-812-4
1. Religion: Christian Life: Inspirational
2. Religion: Christian Life: Spiritual Growth
11.01.04

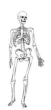

acknowledgments

First to God who dropped this book into my spirit and birthed the idea from there and because of everything I had to face. You let me know I was never alone, and without you this or anything else would not be possible. To my loving and caring husband who believed in me and allowed me the time and space to spread my wings while being one of my biggest supporters and has been by my side during this entire journey. To my father who has loved me and encouraged me along the way to keep my head up and given me priceless advice throughout the entire process and for him allowing God to use him by purchasing my laptop, which has been a gift that will keep on giving. To Grandma Cotton, one who was a prayer warrior in her time that taught me the importance of spending time alone with God and the strength behind it. Then to Grandma Pace, who showed me the importance of godly hospitality and how to care for others through her years of compassion and selflessness. To my special aunt who has always been an inspiration and a treasure to me by truly living out what it means to be a Proverbs 31 woman and taking over from where my mother left off by instilling morals and integrity in me that I still hold dear to this very day. To my mother and father in law for making me feel like I am really part of your family. Thanks for the continued support, prayers, advice and most of all for loving me. Then there is my best friend, who has been more like a soul sister that has never allowed me the opportunity to quit on life by being the one person who has stood by my side through it all, the good and the bad and loved me and never judged me and has only ever wanted the best for me. Then to a lady who is more like my blood cousin instead of an in-law she has been instrumental in praying with me and speaking into my life the things of God and through it all has shown me how to stand even in the face of adversity. To my brother who has shown me that they can lock you up physically but that God can unlock you spiritually and place you on a platform to witness and minister to his people and that obedience is better than sacrifice, and for loving me unconditionally. To my pastor and first lady, who I met during this transition, because they allowed God to use them in showing His glory through their transparency and eye-opening testimonies while all along displaying genuine love and affection one from another. To all the people that I interviewed for the book, thanks for being so candid with me and the readers and allowing me to change your names to protect your identities.

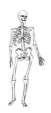

table of contents

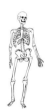

introduction

In this book I hope to contrast with interviews and real talk how Christians are being perceived and allow us to examine ourselves wholeheartedly at what we can do to still be salt and light of this dying world. Are you a "Dead Christian Walking?" Maybe you picked up this book because the title took you by surprise, but like many are unsure of what the title truly means. In this book I hope to answer your questions by taking a different approach with interviews from Christians and non-Christians alike to see how modern day Christians are being perceived and then contrast that with the word of God and see how we score. This book should inspire self-examination and awareness of our true selves and see if we are still being salt and light of this dying world. There are questions that we should all ask ourselves on a daily basis to gage where we are at in our Christian walk. Like am I the same person I was when I first accepted Christ into my life? Our my desires more worldly than Godly? Have I allowed my light to shine so before man? Am I doing all I am capable of when it comes to being an effective witness for Christ? This is the key to help us attract and not distract from bringing lost souls into the kingdom of God. While posing questions to nonbelievers, I was alarmed by the growing number that equates most Christians to be mere hypocrites. When discussing men or women of the cloth with fellow co-workers, they used colorful terms like gangsters, drug dealers, thieves, pimps, hoes, and adulterers. It is time we take a cold, hard look at not only how they perceive us but really look in the mirror and pay attention to the reflection, or shall I say reflections, staring back at us. We were given a charge in the bible to spread the good news. By sharing the word with others we take a role in winning souls for the kingdom. I have to ask if we are still thriving or dying in this area?

There are so many conversations that I witnessed, where people are deciding to stay out of church all together because of what awaits them on the other side of the door. Some have not even gotten that far, they are simply going on what they have seen in people confessing to be Christians and for them that is something so far from what they imagined that they do not want to subject their family or themselves to it. We have to wonder why "church folk" are giving the church as a whole a bad reputation. It is time we address this situation without running away from it but figuring out how we can put our selfish needs aside and allow for God's plan to be carried out in the world. As you are reading this, take a minute to do a self-check and ponder on the question if you have become a hindrance or a help due to your witness? Just think are the people you interact with wanting or desiring a real relationship with God? Are they commenting that they see a change in you that is so awesome that they want that same feeling for themselves? Or do they want nothing to do with the God you serve because your actions have tainted their view altogether? This may be a tougher question to answer than you realized because it means that you have to get real with yourself first. I say that because for many of us we see ourselves being more saved than we really are. So it is difficult for us to take notice of how people respond to our spirituality.

Somewhere along the line, it got a bit blurry for many of us, we began to do what we wanted to do, and we failed to stop and see how this was affecting others around us. There are many of us who grew up in the church, and we have seen so many that came before us carry on the same way, one way in church, and afterwards we wondered where that person went sort of like Dr. Jekyll and Mr. Hyde. We sat by and watched as scandals were brought out about the pastors at many local churches in awe and utter disgust. I have to wonder what part if any does the body of Christ play in being a part of the solution. For far too long we have been an increasingly large part of the problem; because over the years the world's concepts got into the church instead of the church making an inedible impact on this world. While discussing this book with people, I found that mostly everyone had an opinion.

There was one young woman who told that the church sure knows how to preach salvation but no one got up and spoke on how to live out a saved lifestyle. Why is that? Could it be the reason why many get saved join the church and we never hear from them again?

I have to ask; what is the church for each one individually. To some it has become a place to meet and greet, find a spouse, or someone else's for that matter. For others it has become a place to show off their finest threads and to be seen as stylish and fashion forward week after week. You have many who believe they will enter in to heaven simply by their deeds, so they join every ministry and group there is and then feel superior with that religious spirit they have been toting around for years. Then there are those who feel it has become the in thing to do, so it's something we schedule in our planners or put on the calendars as a to-do list, and once we attend, it gets checked off for that day or week we attended. For all the ones mentioned above they feel good, like they accomplished something in that moment regardless if they came out changed, they now have a title "Christian."

The term is used so loosely that just by being amongst a body of believers we all think we fit the category even if the definition states otherwise. The enemy's plan is to keep us in bondage where we never fully come into understanding of God's Word and even then how to apply it to our lives and to walk in what he has purposed for us. Many times we in our natural minds are unable to comprehend how there are divine appointments, even connections that are awaiting us on this journey. How can we get there if we will not put down the mask and the façade long enough to trust that God can deliver us and bring the light into an otherwise darkened existence? People have placed their bets against you to fail on this road and to be another statistic while all along they baited you and waited for your fall; but there is God who has reached out his hand and is waiting for you to stop pretending and playing church and allow him in to change your life and the lives you come in contact with.

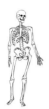

is perception everything?

Have people noticed a change within you? I put this question first because someone other than you should see the difference that Christ has or is making in your everyday life. People who you come in contact with more often should especially notice a change. *Change* referred to in the Hebrew as *Haphak*, haw-fak, is defined in Strong's Dictionary as to turn about or over. To change, overturn, return, pervert, become change, come to be converted. "And do not be conformed to this world, but be transformed by the renewing of your mind, that you may prove what is that good and acceptable and perfect will of God" (Romans 12:2, NKJV). Conformed means "to form" or "mold." The believer should be transformed, that is changed by the renewing of the mind. Do you still hang out at the same places you used to? I am sure you know which ones I am referring to, those old watering holes. Do you still partake in the things of old? We know we are supposed to die to our flesh daily—the question is: have you or do you even attempt to? With every step we take, it is being looked at and scrutinized by others on the outside because more than likely you are the only God they see. So our lives—which by the way are not our own, as much as you would like to say otherwise—need to reflect that we have come into submission of something greater than ourselves.

Is attending worship service every Sunday religiously enough? Or have you actually established a real relationship with our Lord and Savior Jesus Christ? Practicing the religious act of being at church each week without a pure interaction with God is merely just being in attendance. Understanding that we are not to forsake the assembly of ourselves with other believers is indeed important but just showing up and not taking time out to truly build a relationship with Abba, our father is like showing up to college on the first day without having paid your tuition, it just is not enough to get you in. Ask yourself would you in fact recognize his voice if you heard it now? "My sheep hear my voice, and I know them, and they follow me. And I give them eternal life, and they shall never perish; neither shall anyone snatch them out of my hand" (John 10:27–28, NKJV).

Since you have been saved how many people have you brought into the fold? During many conversations the one thing that stood out the most was how babes and mature saints claimed they have had trouble in this area. Could it be that sometimes when given a gift we find it difficult to share the contents of that gift with others? The thing is that we all have been given this charge. Have you taken the time to share your testimonies in hopes of reaching the lost? "Let your light shine before men, that they may see your good works and glorify your Father in heaven" (Matthew 5:16, NKJV). People are always on fire when they first get saved; man, they run out of the church and begin cleaning up the streets until they hit a road block. Then for many it becomes difficult to share the goodness of Jesus when life begins beating you down. It should be enough to witness to others that you are still standing, in spite of your circumstances and adversities. Strength is built in numbers, so if I notice you not being moved, I will want to stand strong too. Staying in commune with Christ and studying the word are essential elements needed on this journey.

Are you totally putting your trust in the Lord or only when it is convenient? Maybe you believe you alone hold the key to your destiny. Have you succumbed to God's will for your life, or are you steadily establishing your will to be priority? "Trust in the Lord with all thine heart, and lean not unto thine own understanding. In all thy ways acknowledge him, and he shall direct thy paths" (Proverbs 3:5–6, KJV). It takes more than just saying you believe and trust God for your outcome. To trust is to have faith, and we all know that faith is an action word. When interviewing saints, it was obvious that many never fully put their faith and trust in the Lord to fully deliver them from their past transgressions. Most of us out here have one foot in the Lord and the other in the world still. Many claim it is too difficult to walk this narrow road. This makes you wonder how many truly have tried to withstand temptation. Sin is the familiar, so for some it may not feel good, but to leave it is too much like right. It becomes like that old shoe; we know the heal is worn down and busting at the soles, but, child, who feels like taming a new pair?

Do you allow the negative perceptions of others around you to darken your outlook? Stop allowing the transference of pessimistic outlooks to come reside in you. What if we allowed every person we come in contact with to shape our image? We would be a walking and ticking time bomb. In terms of your spiritual maturity, it is of the essence to take a hard look at your friends and associates. Ask yourself who is in your inner circle; if it is the "woe is me" crowd, then you need to move on and fast. I understand there are ones that we can lead to Christ and witness to, but many have noticed your progression; but time and again they are feeling down and want you to join them at the bar and get drunk to coax their pain. In reality they get tipsy and the next day awake with the same mess, only this time they are doing it with a hangover, and guess what, so are you! Remember in life we are the company we keep. "Do not be deceived: Evil company corrupts good habits" (1 Corinthians 15:33, NKJV).

Have you truly taken the limits of God, or are you steadily putting limitations on him? Even though God is no respecter of persons, you can't believe him for that same miracle in your own life. God can do more than we can even imagine, so it would be nice if we would stop putting a cap on his ability. Your attitude will determine your altitude, so begin to think outside the box and know that our Lord is capable of the impossible. Stop settling for less than God's best in your life and the lives of others around you. There is nothing worse than when you are trusting God for a miracle and you share that with someone and they take an ax to it. Please keep your unbelief to yourself for I know Jehovah to be a way maker, someone who can say, "Let there be," and it becomes. In many instances, you looked up to that person because of their walk with God, and at that moment if they are not careful, it could damage where you are at and make you feel as if it will not come to pass for you. "Now to him who is able to do exceedingly abundantly above all that we ask or think, according to the power that works in us" (Ephesians 3:20, NKJV).

Are you finding yourself becoming more like the world and less like Christ? First it was watching some soft porn on the idiot tube. You know the one that seems like a reality show but in fact is not fit for you to be watching and salivating over. Or it could be deciding to hang out with the crew that would not know Christ if he showed up while they were getting high or shooting up and he said, "Boo." We constantly place ourselves in sticky situations that tempt our sinful flesh, thinking we are showing them something by us being the only "so-called Christian" in their midst. In all actuality we are playing right into the hand of the enemy by downplaying the obvious. Slowly allowing the devil to get his foot back in our lives, assuming we are in control, when all along we have been relinquishing our power right over. "When I was a child, I spoke like a child, thought like a child, and reasoned like a child. When I became a man, I gave up my childish ways" (1 Corinthians 13:11, ISV).

Does your life display a life of holiness and righteousness or only when someone is watching? When I say someone, I mean other believers. Putting on a godly act, making others think you have truly changed when in fact the only changing you have done is the undergarments you put on this week. Yet you run around with impressionable nonbelievers who were getting excited about the new you till the old you showed up wanting to partake in their lifestyle. Now they have labeled you a hypocrite and put you on the list with the rest. Then you wonder why they can never come to Christ, they have not been shown a good example for watching you and your hidden sins over the years. "That the triumphing of the wicked is short, and the joy of the hypocrite is but for a moment" (Job 20:5, NKJV).

Did you first perceive this walk to be easy or one that you would follow when it was working for you? Following the leader is always convenient when life is looking up, but the moment the water gets troubled, we are back to taking a page out of the gospel according to ourselves. You know what I am talking about; it would be like me taking a scripture out of St. Bullock 1:1. Nothing in life worth having will truly come easy. We have to work at it on a daily basis, embrace change, and get into the word, which will be like meat for our souls. If you run out of gas and there is nothing in your reserve, how much farther do you suppose you will go? Same is true with having the word down on the inside but then not just attending Sunday worship but coming on Wednesday to get that extra to carry you through the rest of the week while meditating on.

During your trials and tribulations was the outcome ever having your character strengthened?

> We can rejoice, too, when we run into problems and trials, for we know that they help us develop endurance. And endurance develops strength of character, and character strengthens our confident hope of salvation.
>
> Romans 5:3, NLT

Not just going through your trials and tribulations, but coming out with a steadfast and unmovable mindset is key. Your integrity and morals are now lifting a standard. The greater the tribulation, the greater the blessing; so even when it seems like all odds are against you, that is when you should press in even further. Through it all, we should be thanking and praising God for what is being ushered into our lives.

At what point do we begin to assume responsibility for the way the world perceives Christians? I have noticed with some reality shows they will have a person claiming to be a "Christian" and everything they do is in contradiction to that. One said, "Just because I like to get drunk and party that doesn't have anything to do with my religion because the two are separate entities and people should stop trying to put them together." . I thought, many times this thinking can be deemed as a problem especially in witnessing to unbelievers. We will claim to be a Christian when it suits, but in many instances we do not want that minor formality associated with our lifestyle. Almost as if life can continue as it always has until my day of worship. Man, that even made me smirk a little bit there, because this is what nonbelievers see us do and be honest what is the difference at that point between us and them? All the perks without any of the hard work, wouldn't you say? We know as Christians that it is okay to drink reasonably and not to be a drunkard. Paul describes in the Bible that to view freedom in Christ can be used as a selfish opportunity for the flesh and that he does not believe we should do that or be a stumbling block for our brothers.

> For you have been called to live in freedom, my brothers and sisters. But don't use your freedom to satisfy your sinful nature. Instead, use your freedom to serve one another in love.
>
> Galatians 5:13, NLT

> But you must be careful so that your freedom does not cause others with a weaker conscience to stumble.
>
> 1 Corinthians 8:9, NLT

Would people identify you to be a Christian in the workplace? Or are you a closet Christian that only allows your spirituality out at home or on Sundays? During my interviews, I found that there were many closet Christians. They have begun to allow the personalities in the workplace to shape them and not vice versa. You have to wonder why they are allowing their light not to shine. We begin partaking in their conversations, and never do we take a stand for what we know to be right. Maybe they think they will be alone in this pursuit, but is that reason enough to just say nothing? We spend the majority of our day at work and around coworkers. Suddenly their music is permeating the atmosphere and their thoughts are becoming ours. Cursing even seems like the norm around them, so we let a few slip to feel accepted. Ask yourself: has God called us to be accepted in this way, or are we to be set apart and made holy and prayerfully we can win them over by the God in us?

> Work hard so you can present yourself to God and receive his approval. Be a good worker, one who does not need to be ashamed and who correctly explains the word of truth. Avoid worthless, foolish talk that only leads to more godless behavior.
>
> 2 Timothy 2:15–16, NLT

Since you have been saved, have you truly seen the hand of God at work in your life? Has it been evident in where you have seen mountains moved due to the prayers you have prayed, or situations changed for the better all the while receiving his unmerited favor upon you? I believe as saints we need to know God to be true to his word; there should be experiences where he has been instrumental in healing our bodies or able to restore relationships we knew to be loss. Our Heavenly Father has the ability to open and close doors that will place us closer to our destiny. What does God call us to do as Christians?

Would you consider yourself to be a "lazy Christian"? You get upset about how they are taking God out of the classrooms through prayer, out of government and practically everywhere else. When the news gets to your door or inbox, how does it impact you? Are you quick to hit send and gossip among yourselves how this is wrong, but then the bubble you reside in never implodes. Or maybe you say, "What can my words or petitions actually do to stop this from happening? We are fine sitting in the pews but never evoking real change." Have you tapped into the knowledge that we can go boldly before the throne? We must make our petitions known to Christ. Then we must get off our soapbox and write to our congressmen/women and see what we can do in our own cities and states across this great nation. Spiritual warfare is real, and we should attack it as such. "Behold, I give you the authority to trample on serpents and scorpions, and over all the power of the enemy, and nothing shall by any means hurt you" (Luke 10:19, NKJV). This is our time to use what God has given us and begin to be bold and declare authority over the workings of the enemy.

Have you cast down strongholds or generational curses that plague you and your family? Many of us are not targeting specific areas in our lives and the lives of others that the Word says should be done with praying and fasting. Many of us are walking around with curses that have been deeply rooted in our families for years, and the sad part is we repeat the sin in our own life, and now it has wings to continue on because we didn't take a stand and say, "No more; this curse stops here." Imagine if we all stood up and went to war with the enemy and let him know that he can't have our lives because we decided to put an end to this once and for all.

Paul described strongholds as anything that exalts itself against the knowledge of God.

> For though we walk in the flesh, we do no war according to the flesh. For the weapons of our warfare are not carnal but mighty in God for pulling down strongholds, casting down arguments and every high thing that exalts itself against the knowledge of God, bringing every thought into captivity to the obedience of Christ.
>
> 2 Corinthians 10:3–5, NKJV

God gave us as believer's authority over the enemy, so why are we not using it? How many of us have joined with others in the body of Christ and begun prayer groups where we actually tackle together things or areas afflicting our families or churches? Do you honestly pray for your pastors/leaders? We must lift them up even before going into the house of the Lord. Prayer can begin at home that week, so you can be expecting an incredible outcome of souls being delivered and set free. God is still in the *saving business*, you know. God sent his only son, Jesus, to save a dying world. It is something to see that we are becoming an extinct breed. Or could it be that you do not care as long as you make it in to heaven? I want to get to heaven too, but I want to do it knowing that I not only lived for God but tried my best to impact the lost and expect to see them there as well. This is one of the many things I love about God—there is more than enough of him to go around. There is no need to feel like you have to keep him all to yourself; please pass his love along.

What about your government? Have you taken a moment out of your day from complaining about the state of affairs to kneeling down and praying that God direct the path of the president and the other elected officials? Many people feel as if their voice will never be heard, but I beg to differ with you try the Father and see if he won't hear you. The way we make a difference is to put our faith into action, not just sitting and allowing it to lie dormant. Also praying a hedge of protection for President Obama is key since he has encountered the most death threats of any United States president.[1]

Do you find yourself still lying to the people you claim to care about? Maybe you think that it is for their own good that you continue to lie to them so that their feelings will not get hurt, when in all actuality it not only hurts them but it will have a gross impact on your walk with God. God is a God that operates in spirit and in truth. Lying stinks and is an awful aroma and scent that is displeasing to the nostrils of God. Sin separates us from the Father, so why is it that we as Christians still tell lies and think that our anointing is still intact?

> There are six things which the Lord hates, yes, seven which are an abomination to him: Haughty eyes, a lying tongue, and hands that shed innocent blood, a heart that devises wicked plans, feet that run rapidly to evil, a false witness who utters lies, and one who spreads strife among brothers.
>
> Proverbs 6:16–19, NASB

Are there moral obligations you think you have as a Christian? What about when it comes to the law of the land? Do you obey the speed limit? I myself used to be a person who raced to get to places and did not always adhere to the speed limit, and it took me getting a ticket, and things spiraled from there, and I knew that I was being taught a lesson of obeying the law of the land. To some that might not seem like much, but when you have relocated somewhere and funds are tight and you have been waiting till you get a new church home to tithe again, you begin to learn multiple teachings all at once.

Do you believe that infidelity is a sin or only if you get caught? Have you been unfaithful to your spouse? Are you known to practice deception in your relationship? Are believers exchanging integrity just to be accepted by their so-called peers? Maybe you think there is plenty of time to get in line with the word of God and as for now you can just have fun and ask for forgiveness later. In an instant everything in your life can change and what if there was never a tomorrow for you to get it right?

We should be walking in victory; instead so many of us go around in a defeated frame of mind. Why are there more saved women than men, especially in the homes? And then we are raising our kids up to see that there is no real urgency to get our lives in order. Some feel they have plenty of time because of others they have seen out here. Days are getting less, and people are dying younger and younger, and none of us know the day or the time or second that we will go away from here and yet we wait till most times it is too late.

Honestly ask yourself if you have interfered with others coming to Christ, maybe with your negative attitude or lack of faith in God. You know the type—nothing ever goes your way, which you constantly remind people of. You cannot believe God to pay your bills much less fix your marriage, get you a job, or heal your loved ones. Looking from the outside in, it appears to them that being a Christian is a bunch of doom and gloom. Man, they are always trying to cheer you up and give you a dollar, and you wonder why they never except your offer to attend service especially since you have five bumper stickers on your ride that read "Try Jesus." Shucks, they are waiting for you to really *try Jesus* and then get back to them with some results.

We have to be ever so careful in our interactions with others by making sure we are not spewing scriptures one minute and then cursing them out the next. Sometimes if we could just stop and think of the impact we are having on nonbelievers and ourselves for that matter. We are not growing as mature Christians because we are saved but not delivered. Here we are still walking around with the same baggage we had before coming to God just with a new title in front of our names, Sister So and So—you know what I mean. Then on Sundays we steadily pray for pews to be filled, not seeing that numbers without substance are just numbers. Might as well call them seat fillers because they are no real bother to the enemy's camp because we are not shaking the foundation and he knows we are just going to keep complaining and never do anything to change our circumstances. "But do you want to know, O foolish man, that faith without works is dead?" (James 2:20, NKJV).

Or maybe we are running people off by being too critical when they step foot in the church house. Instead of showing them Christ, who is love, we show them how we back bite, gossip, and do anything short of lending an encouraging word. Too often we are worried about what they have on, something is too skimpy, how dare they, oh man look at all that makeup and those big earrings, things that run them away. Why not put a sign outside that reads "Only people that have it together can attend our worship service because all you sinners and heathens stay clear." I thought the house of God was supposed to be inviting where the sinners came to get right not to be shunned away and talked about. God did say, "Come as you are," so we should allow them to enter in and allow time for them to receive the Holy Spirit, which will then be their guide. It is sad that our reputation precedes us in a negative light everywhere we go.

Many people are scared to be labeled as a "Christian." They feel that it has a negative connotation linked to it. Most see us as unapproachable, which discourages them from wanting to get to close to us. Some think it's necessary to walk on eggshells around us because we are always being too critical of them and their behavior. Would you want to be around people that judge you before you even attempt to open your mouth and say hello? So many of us are set on church traditions instead of saving souls, and then we happen to look up one day to find pews empty and all we have left is our manmade traditions. There are more people hurting sitting up in the church house week to week and many never seem to get what they are looking for. If you look closely, you can see and feel the coldness between different saints that have nothing to do about God. What work at the point are we doing? Looks like our own agenda again. Then we have the ones at church posted up simply to lure someone in to their web of lust even if they are married, we still want what someone else has, and somehow we conjure up that we are being godly about it. Let's take a cold, hard look at how the world really perceives us in the next chapter.

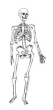

interviews with non-christians

Subject: Justin, single male in his midtwenties.

Me: Would you consider yourself to be a Christian?

Justin: No I would not say I was a Christian.

Me: Have you ever attended church?

Justin: Yes, I grew up in church and was there for a large portion of my life.

Me: Do you have a local assembly that you worship at regularly?

Justin: Not at this time. I go here and there.

Me: Are you considering joining?

Justin: Not really.

Me: Is there a reason why?

Justin: It's hard to have a desire to join any church at the moment due to the fact that there are so many pastors that frequent my local establishment.

Me: Your local establishment? Do you mean you see them all the time where you reside at?

Justin: Not quite like that. Every now and again I dibble and dabble in selling some street narcotics, and there are a few pastors here in town that are regular patrons.

Me: Wait, are you saying that they purchase drugs from you every now and then?

Justin: More often than that, and I find it difficult to join church when this is what the pastors are doing.

Me: Well, there are other churches. Could you go to one of them?

Justin: I will wait because I do not want to play with God, so until I get myself all the way together, I will just remain the same.

Me: I understand what you are saying about being genuine, but there is something you should know: God does not require you to come to him once you have it all together, but he is waiting with open arms right now and loves you and wants to help you along the way. No pressure. Just keep that in mind, and thanks for being very open and honest.

Subject: Manny, single man in midtwenties who at one time wanted to be saved but perception diminished by seeing so-called Christians he knows personally.

Me: Have you noticed a difference in Christians than with the rest of the world?

Manny: Most of them are not setting good examples. They talk dirty, speak their minds, and will curse you out in a heartbeat. They only refer to the Bible as it suits for others. But they in fact live outside of that themselves.

Me: Do you have direct examples to back up your statement above?

Manny: Yes, I have witnessed Christians I know going to the clubs on Saturdays and then going home with different individuals and sleeping with them and then showing up for church the next day and singing in the choir as if they are holy and saved.

Me: What about the pastors? Do you see Christ in them?

Manny: About 60 percent of pastors are somewhat good, but most bend the truth and interpret the Bible passages to be different than what it should.

Me: What do you think it is to be a Christian?

Manny: To base your life/religion off Christ, by making sacrifices and changes to do these things. Live beyond the line even if it affects you. If you fall, then get back up again and get back in line.

Me: I appreciate your time and honesty.

Subject: Jim, single man in his late forties that feels Christians are phony.

Me: Do you feel there is a difference between Christians and the rest of the world?

Jim: No, I can't see a difference because they live their lives as the rest of the world does.

Me: What is your opinion of Christians?

Jim: I feel that they use that term loosely, some are hypocrites. They do not practice what they go around preaching.

Me: Thanks for sharing with us your views on Christians.

Subject: Sadie, divorced female in her early forties, not saved.

Me: From the Christians you know, do you think they are different from the rest of the world?

Sadie: No, a lot say it, but they do not live their lives any differently.

Me: Explain in your own words some of the behavior they exhibit.

Sadie: Many of them still go to clubs and party and drink heavily and then attend worship services on Sunday morning acting holier than thou.

Me: How do you think Christians are supposed to act?

Sadie: I feel they should be serving God in a manner that does not just mean going to church on Sundays. They should read their Bibles and be a servant like Christ.

Me: Do you find it difficult to believe people when they claim to be Christians?

Sadie: Yes, because only a few really are and have that actual understanding where the others are mere hypocrites.

Me: What understanding are you speaking of in general?

Sadie: One where it has to come from within you and not be displayed as a superficial service at best. Main goal should be to serve God.

Me: Thanks for being open and honest with your views.

Subject: Anthony, married male in his late thirties, nonbeliever.

Me: Have you noticed any differences in Christians versus the rest of the world?

Anthony: No, lots of Christians live just like the world does.

Me: Can you elaborate on that theory?

Anthony: Yes, all humans, whatever their environment, will soon adapt to it. You need to have people around you with similar beliefs.

Me: So without a similar belief system, what do you feel will begin to happen?

Anthony: Well, for instance, in the churches I have been to, you see that half the deacons are having sexual relations with most of the front row and then the pastors have the choirs on lockdown.

Me: Do you think that is being too harsh about the pastors?

Anthony: Well I do not believe the pastors started out that way.

Me: What way are you pertaining to?

Anthony: As crooks, thieves and gangsters. I think they got this way when offerings began to get bigger they began to get tempted by their flesh.

Me: So do you feel that pastors should not get offerings or reap from this at all?

Anthony: I believe they should reap rewards of it but not require or even ask their members to bring in their tax papers and W2s; it's just ridiculous. That is where the greed takes over and they want it all.

Me: What are some more behaviors that you saw from Christians that lined up with the world's views?

Anthony: Well, just from attending different churches and never being saved myself, I pretty much felt I was the same way they were.

Me: What do you mean by that?

Anthony: Well, my cousin and I would run into the women at church that said they were Christians, and we would sleep with them and then see them at the clubs just like anyone else. We slept with a lot of so-called saved women at a variety of churches.

Me: I appreciate you being very candid with your depiction of what you encountered firsthand.

interviews with christians

Subject: Sanchez, in his early twenties, married, and has been saved for five years.

Me: In your own words, explain the change that has occurred in you since you have been saved.

Sanchez: I do not judge people as much. I used to dictate how I would treat them by that. Stopped smoking and now all of my friends are saved so I didn't have to stop hanging out with them. I cover my household now, and I have a good personal relationship with God. I believe he is happy with me at the end of each day. Because I am no longer of the world, I now make a conscious effort to change daily.

Me: Are there still things that you did before you were saved that you fall into now as well?

Sanchez: I still party, drink occasionally, only a social drinker now, flirt still, still listen to secular music, and I still find myself lying.

Me: Have you taken the charge to win souls for Christ?

Sanchez: Yes.

Me: When trials and tribulations come, do you stay down or get back up and stay on the path?

Sanchez: I allow it to strengthen my character.

Me: Would you say that people see a change in you?

Sanchez: Yes, I think people notice a difference in me from how I used to be.

Me: Do you think you are sold out for Christ?

Sanchez: Yes.

Me: Is there anything you would like to leave me with?

Sanchez: I would like you to ask people if they were arrested and had to go to on trial for being saved, would they have enough evidence to convict you?

Me: Thanks for your time.

Subject: Willie, single man in his early fifties, has been saved for ten years.

Me: In your own words, explain the change that has occurred in you since you have been saved.

Willie: First off, I believe I was saved by grace, and I still sin. I have begun developing a personal relationship with God—something I didn't have before.

Me: Are there still things that you did before you were saved that you fall into now as well?

Willie: There are times that I slip up and curse. I don't drink anymore because that was a vice that God delivered me from since I was an alcoholic in the past. My biggest struggle is having sexual intercourse outside of marriage being that I am single, but I don't feel that this will have an effect on my salvation or me going to heaven.

Me: Have you taken the charge to win souls for Christ?

Willie: I am growing in this area. I know that I am to be salt and light, just not walking in it yet at this time.

Me: When trials and tribulations come, do you stay down or get back up and stay on the path?

Willie: I try to encourage myself often, and when I get down, I like to take a look at what God has previously brought me through, and that gives me strength to continue on because God is faithful.

Me: Would you say that people see a change in you?

Willie: Definitely, from the man I used to be when I was in the world.

Me: Do you think you are sold out for Christ?

Willie: Indeed.

Me: Is there anything you would like to leave me with?

Willie: If you aren't being spiritually fed in a church, I feel that you should find another church home because it is time to move on.

Me: Thanks for your time.

Subject: Brittney, who is a married mother of three and has been saved for over twenty years and in her late forties.

Me: In your own words, explain the change that has occurred in you since you have been saved.

Brittany: I am now more conscious of how I do things and to my reactions in situations too. Most people felt I was always a goody two-shoes even before I was saved.

Me: Are there still things that you did before you were saved that you fall into now as well?

Brittany: I still will find myself in a lie from time to time but not often. I never cursed or smoked; I drank a little, but I no longer indulge in that.

Me: Have you taken the charge to win souls for Christ?

Brittany: Yes, I feel it is infectious.

Me: Is your husband a Christian?

Brittany: He says that he is. He was saved about ten years ago.

Me: Does he attend church with you and the kids?

Brittany: He only attended twice since he has been saved, and two out of the three children go, but it is hard getting them to go when they see he doesn't want to come.

Me: Twice in ten years. Well, does he edify himself with Christian things?

Brittany: No, he doesn't read his Word, he does not listen to gospel music, nor does he watch any Christian television.

Me: How does this impact you?

Brittany: It affects me very deeply; I know some things we go through in our marriage would be different if he took his rightful place in God. Also it would help the children to see both of their parents living a holy lifestyle.

I think it would be nice for my husband to cover not only me but the entire household in prayer daily.

Me: I appreciate your openness. Have a great day.

Subject: Lamar is a married man and a father of two in his late thirties saved for ten years.

Me: Are there things that you no longer do now that you are saved?

Lamar: I no longer smoke, drink, nor do I flirt or attend bars/clubs anymore.

Me: What about areas that you still struggle in occasionally if any?

Lamar: I have found myself cursing from time to time, and lying as well.

Me: How do you see yourself as being set apart from the world?

Lamar: I believe I am peculiar, now I have a distinguishing attribute. I believe my actions speak louder than any words I could say. I have a personal relationship with my savior now, and I believe I am sold out to Him.

Me: What about in the work place, are you winning them over or have you succumb to their ways?

Lamar: I do believe that there has been a transfer of spirit from them to me.

Me: In what ways—if you do not mind sharing with us?

Lamar: I have begun cursing like them and taking part in conversations that I would not normally allow myself to be a part of.

Me: Do you think you are a closeted Christian?

Lamar: Yes, because most people I work with do not even know that I am a Christian.

Me: In that, do you think you are being an effective witness?

Lamar: No, because I have picked up on their ways, and now my light is not shining as much lately.

Me: What do you think God is calling for right now?

Lamar: I think that this economical shift is a wakeup call for people to see that we cannot put our trust in the economy or the government, but we need to be bringing people to Christ.

Me: Do you have enough saltiness to attract people to Christ right now?

Lamar: No, not enough I have to do better.

Me: Thanks for your cooperation during this interview.

Subject: Kenney, who is a married man that has been saved for nine years and married for twelve years.

Me: I notice you said you have been married for twelve years and out of those years you have only been saved for nine of them. Is that the same for your spouse?

Kenney: No, my spouse was saved during the entire time.

Me: Do you feel that not being equally yoked made it harder for your marriage back then?

Kenney: Yes, it was much harder because we were both learning one another as well. It became very overwhelming.

Me: In what ways did it become that?

Kenney: Well, I used to put my family before my wife, and I would tell them things and get their advice and not hers in many situations.

Me: I can imagine that made the relationship very difficult because you did not see your spouse as being one with you.

Kenney: True indeed, I took that bond for granted because I did not know any better till I got saved myself.

Me: Would you share with us how being saved changed your marriage?

Kenney: It taught me how God wanted me to treat my wife. It has made our marriage closer, we began knowing how the other was actually feeling before it even came out of the other's mouth.

Me: Would people consider you to be a closet Christian?

Kenney: No, they know I live for God.

Me: Have you taken the charge to win souls for the kingdom?

Kenney: I have tried to fulfill it, but I can do better.

Me: Thanks for your time and allowing us to see the difference being saved made in your marriage.

Subject: Robert, a single male in his late twenties who has been saved for fourteen years.

Me: Do you attend church regularly, Robert?

Robert: Not as much as I used to, once or twice every month since I relocated; but when I go home I attend regularly.

Me: Do you have a church home in the state you relocated to?

Robert: No, I do not, just one I go to all the time.

Me: How long has it been since you relocated?

Robert: I have been here for three years.

Me: Is there a reason that you have not joined a church here?

Robert: I am not looking for membership, just the Word; I still am a member of my church in my home state.

Me: In your own words, explain or describe the change that has occurred in you since you have been saved.

Robert: I have more of a desire to do the right thing now than before.

Me: Are there still things that you did before you were saved that you fall into now as well?

Robert: I still smoke, drink. Instead of clubbing, I go to the strip clubs and bars now.

Me: Do you date a lot being that you are a single, accomplished man?

Robert: There is a moderate level of dating happening in my life right now.

Me: Do you have pre-marital sex?

Robert: Yes, I do.

Me: Do you date other Christians?

Robert: Most of the time, I date other Christians. Not looking to date women that do not believe in God.

Me: Have you dated married women since you have been saved?

Robert: Yes, I have dated married women and slept with them.

Me: What do you think is the difference between Christians and non-Christians?

Robert: Mainly just our beliefs, but everything else is mainly the same.

Me: Is there anything that you do not like about the church as a whole?

Robert: I feel that mega churches are a bit impersonal; also I notice Christians behaving one way in church and then another way outside of church.

Me: Are you a tither?

Robert: No, I am not a tither.

Me: Do you feel forced to give at churches?

Robert: No, not at all.

Me: When do you think you will get a stronger walk with God?

Robert: I have been putting it on the back burner; I have not really gotten totally into it, and there is no set time or set age that I will.

Me: Have you taken the charge to win souls for the kingdom?

Robert: Not voluntarily to strangers, but more so to the people I know, I try to lead by being an example.

Me: Do you think you are sold out to Christ?

Robert: I think I am partially sold out.

Me: Would you say that people see a change in you?

Robert: Some notice a difference.

Me: Would you say that you are a closet Christian?

Robert: I am a little bit of a closet Christian; most people would be surprised if they knew because of things that I have done with them or around them.

Me: I really appreciate your being transparent with me.

Subject: Christie, single lady in her early twenties, has been saved off and on the last seven years, and lives with her boyfriend and daughter.

Me: When you say off and on for the last seven years, what do you actually mean?

Christie: Well, I would go to churches and get saved, and then I would have a problem with staying saved.

Me: So basically you have been a back slider and you have rededicated yourself back to Christ?

Christie: Yes.

Me: Have you changed since you first received Christ in your life?

Christie: The first year I was on fire and after that no.

Me: In what ways have you stopped?

Christie: I do not attend church as often, I like to party and drink, and I am having sex outside of marriage.

Me: Do you feel that this makes you different from other Christians?

Christie: No, because people use that term too loosely in this day and age.

Me: Why do you think that is?

Christie: I think they are a lot like me they are very excited at first, and then they begin to run cold.

Me: Do you have a personal relationship with God?

Christie: No, I do not; I have never had that feeling to begin one.

Me: Okay, and you still call yourself a Christian?

Christie: Yes, I do.

Me: Thanks for taking time out to be open and honest with me.

Subject: John is a married man in his early thirties with no kids and has been saved for five years.

Me: In your own words, explain or describe the change that has occurred in you since you have been saved.

John: I pray more than I used to, and I cut out certain things from my life.

Me: Are there still things that you did before you were saved that you fall into now as well?

John: Yes, I still smoke cigarettes; I smoke marijuana occasionally and drink too. I still lust after females, and lying is a problem too.

Me: Have you taken the charge to win souls for the kingdom?

John: I started out that way, but then along the way I stopped.

Me: What has been the hardest part for you with trying to live a saved lifestyle?

John: Letting go of my former self.

Me: Are you a closet Christian?

John: In some form, I would say yes because one moment I may say things pertaining to being a Christian but then I live quite differently.

Me: When trials and tribulations come, do you stay down or get back up and stay on the path, or does it have any effect on you at all?

John: It affects me mainly due to me wanting to do my will instead of God's will and trying to make it happen myself.

Me: Would you say that people see a change in you?

John: Some do see a change as far as family due to them being farther away than the people who see me daily who I sometimes still engage in things with.

Me: Do you think you are sold out to Christ?

John: No, I could do better.

Me: Is your mate saved, and if so, for how long?

John: Yes, my wife is saved and has been since she was young, but she rededicated her life seven years ago.

Me: Does your spouse live a lifestyle that shows Christ?

John: Yes, my wife does.

Me: Were you saved before you got married?

John: I had gotten saved prior to dating my wife, but then I was in a backslidden state after that.

Me: Do you think it is important to be equally yoked?

John: Yes, because in our marriage, there have been times when we were not and that created a pull and tug and then I began to hide things from my spouse because she was living for Christ and I was not.

Me: What have you been saved from?

John: Things of this world.

Me: Do you invite people to church?

John: Yes, I do.

Me: Do you still flirt?

John: Yes, from time to time.

Me: Have you had an affair?

John: No, I have not had an affair.

Me: What about an emotional affair?

John: Yes, I have had emotional affairs.

Me: Why do you think you had emotional affairs being that you are married?

John: Because I never actually let go of the past, and I allowed that soul tie to become a person that I went to when I needed the familiar. Then others because I wanted to show my wife I could do what I wanted to do that she could not tell me what to do with having these women friends basically I had a rebellious spirit.

Me: Do you regret it in any way?

John: Yes, I do regret it because I thought it was me being grown, and I had seen others do this in my family before me so I figured it was okay to repeat the pattern.

Me: Do you still hide things from your spouse?

John: Yes, sometimes I still hide things from my wife.

Me: Do you watch or look at pornography?

John: I used to before I was delivered from it.

Me: During your marriage?

John: Yes, I used to hide it in the house where I figured my wife would not look.

Me: Do you masturbate?

John: I have but not anymore.

Me: If you were on trial for being saved, would they have enough evidence to convict you of being saved?

John: No, they would not.

Me: Do you think that the people claiming to be Christians are giving Christianity as a whole a bad reputation?

John: Yes, I do.

Me: Any last words or comments?

John: I hope my being honest and transparent can really help others to see where they are at in Christ too and change for the better.

Me: I would like to say thank you for opening up to the readers and myself by being so candid.

Subject: Michael, married man in his early forties that has been saved for over twenty-plus years.

Me: Have you changed a lot since you have been saved?

Michael: Yes, I feel I have.

Me: In what type of ways have you changed the most?

Michael: With paying tithes I feel especially.

Me: By doing that, how does it make you feel?

Michael: It makes me feel that I am being obedient and I also believe in following the law of the land too.

Me: Have you won souls for Christ?

Michael: No, I have not done that part, and I feel bad about that.

Me: So in over twenty years, you have not been effective in winning souls?

Michael: I know it is bad to say, but I am a lazy Christian.

Me: Why do you call yourself that?

Michael: Because I know God is not happy with me in the way I am with certain areas of my walk.

Me: Are there some things you still find yourself doing that the world does?

Michael: Yes, I still lie a lot.

Me: Do you feel that it is important that Christians live the lifestyle described in the Word?

Michael: I think the most important thing is that we do God's will.

Me: I am thankful for you sharing with me your views.

Subject: Andy, divorced male, Christian, in late forties, and has been saved for fifteen years.

Me: Do you think that since you have been saved you act differently now?

Andy: Yes, I definitely do.

Me: In what ways have you noticed a change?

Andy: I am a lot calmer now and not concerned with other people's judgment. I do not smoke, and I refuse to lie.

Me: Do you still partake in some things that you used to before turning your life over?

Andy: Yes, I drink from time to time, and I still go to bars and party just nothing wild now. I still have strongholds that I need to be delivered from.

Me: Have your friends noticed a change within you?

Andy: Yes, but I no longer hang out with the same crowd that I used to.

Me: Do you find it difficult being divorced to restrain from having sex outside of marriage now?

Andy: It is hard, but my self-worth has changed, so I am not engaging in sex outside of marriage.

Me: Are you passionate about this upcoming election?

Andy: Yes, very much so.

Me: Are you that passionate about Christ?

Andy: No, I have not been.

Me: Do you think you are being salt and light to this world?

Andy: It often comes up in conversations, but I am not actively recruiting people.

Me: Thanks for your time.

Subject: Jill is a wife and mother of four in her midthirties that has been saved for three years.

Me: In your own words, could you describe the change that has occurred in you since you have been saved?

Jill: I now have a new sense of direction and purpose that has made me aware that I am not to be self-absorbed anymore. God is the head of my life, and I am submitting to His will instead of my own. The outcome has been greater than I could have ever imagined.

Me: Are there still things that you did before you were saved that you fall into now as well?

Jill: I still smoke cigarettes and listen to secular music, and I do not attend church enough either. I feel sometimes that I am not saved or delivered enough because I allow my husband to dictate us going to service on Sundays. I follow him because he is the head and we are in covenant together.

Me: Have you taken the charge to win souls for Christ?

Jill: Yes, I speak about it in almost every conversation; it always comes back to that for me. I have not sought out strangers though.

Me: Would you describe yourself as a closet Christian?

Jill: No.

Me: When trials and tribulations come in your life, what effect does it have on you and your walk with God?

Jill: I have allowed emotions to take me over at times, then I often have to get back in line with him and his will for me by understanding that it comes to make me stronger.

Me: Would you say that people see a change in you?

Jill: Yes, I would say that because my husband sees the love of God in me now; before that I was unable to accept any man's love in a committed relationship. He also knows because I no longer talk, live, or do things the same way.

Me: Do you think you are sold out for Christ?

Jill: Yes.

Me: Is your mate saved, and if so, for how long?

Jill: He says he is, but nothing about him has changed. He still curses, drinks, smokes, and does not want us to attend church.

Me: So you have kids but none attend church?

Jill: Only a number of times have we all went.

Me: With your mate claiming Christianity but not living it in your opinion how do you feel this affects your marriage or household?

Jill: By him not submitting fully under God, it has impacted our household adversely. Obviously the first way is because he will not allow us to attend church due to his negative perception of the institution of church. He believes in spirituality but not organized religion. I feel that our blessings as a whole are being held up. For the most part he is in line with his own will.

Me: What are his reasons for having this negative perception?

Jill: Basically he feels that they are all hypocrites and that they are thieves by always pushing offerings and living off the people of the church.

Me: Did you become a Christian before you were married or after?

Jill: After.

Me: Do you feel that you two should be equally yoked?

Jill: Yes, that is what the Word says because it is extremely hard without it. We deal with enough personal strongholds and generational curses on our own, and it makes it difficult to deal with someone else's especially when they think they are living right.

Me: What have you been saved from?

Jill: I have been saved and delivered from thievery, fornication, lusting after men and money, vanity, drugs and alcohol, pornography, lying/deceiving, and manipulation.

Me: Have you ever invited people to church?

Jill: No because I do not have a church home, so I just tell people to make sure they go to a church.

Me: Do you still flirt even though you are married?

Jill: No.

Me: Have you an affair?

Jill: No.

Me: What about an emotional affair?

Jill: No.

Me: Have you hidden things from your spouse?

Jill: Yes.

Me: Do you watch or look at pornography?

Jill: Not anymore; I have been delivered from that.

Me: Do you masturbate?

Jill: Not anymore; I have been delivered from that as well.

Me: If you were on trial for being saved, would they have enough evidence to convict you?

Jill: Yes, I believe so.

Me: Do you think that people claiming to be Christians give Christianity a bad rap as a whole?

Jill: Yes and no, because we are supposed to be living examples of Christ, and die to our sinful ways daily. I partially blame the church, most are coming from the church and that is why a lot of Christians do not want to attend because of that. Babes in Christ look to mature Christians to set the example of how we are to live our lives. Not to use this excuse because we have to seek Christ for ourselves, but when so many people are broken, they look to their leaders or people they know have been saved for years for direction. Instead they find them gossiping, cursing, and looking down on nonbelievers, and they become hypocrites and then your faith is shaken. When you are new and see this, it makes it that much harder to think God can truly save you. That is why we should seek him first and know his Word. We all struggle, but when broken people come to be healed and you see Christians that look good from the outside but then later learn the ugly truth, it is disheartening. You also see the pastors driving expensive cars and having expensive houses and you are driving in Yugos, you then wonder where your offering is going.

Me: Thanks for sharing your thoughts and time. I appreciate it.

Subject: Louise, divorced female mother of three, has been saved for thirty-three years.

Me: Describe the change that has occurred in you since you became a Christian.

Louise: Over the years, I have grown into it where it has become not so much what I want but what pleases Christ by crucifying self. I pray that I would be godly in all that I do. Even at work I am not working for that person but doing it unto the Lord. I have a different mindset than the world. Old person does not come up as much anymore. More natural, I now live life to please the Father. I try to reflect what I have been taught because many times we are the only God people see, and I want to show his radiant light. I used to have a bad temper, a sensitive nature, and I now try to keep it under control by fasting and praying. Lord, not my will, but your will be done in me. I want to help others by not being so selfish and focused on me. I try to keep my flesh under subjection by allowing spirit man to be built up.

Me: Are there still things that you find yourself falling into that you did even before you were saved?

Louise: No, because for one I did not have a lot of worldly vices in the first place to overcome. Just temperament but I have overcome that. I was never a smoker or drinker.

Me: Have you taken the charge to win souls for Christ?

Louise: I am not one who goes out and stands on street corners and preaches, but I have been out to witness with evangelistic teams, but I try to witness with my conduct on a daily basis. I pray that God gives me a word for someone if they are in need of prayer. I want to live a life so people can accept a word from me.

Me: Are you a closet Christian?

Louise: No.

Me: How do you respond to trials and tribulations that come your way?

Louise: They affect me, because I am still human. I will get back up and rely on my faith and trust in God. The way I fight now is by being on my knees in prayer. Warfare is not carnal so I rely on the Word of God.

Me: Have people noticed a change in you?

Louise: Yes, my family who has known me the longest has seen a change in me. I believe people see a consistency here. They would be shocked if they ever saw me using profanity or being belligerent.

Me: Would you say that you are sold out for Christ?

Louise: Yes.

Me: When you were married, was your mate saved as well?

Louise: Yes, my mate was saved, but then he was in a backslidden state.

Me: Do you have kids that attend service?

Louise: Yes, they all do.

Me: How did the impact of your mate becoming back-slidden affect your union and the household all together?

Louise: My mate had backslidden during the marriage, which caused a damper on our situation with the way we raised the children. You want to adhere to the teaching that you both were following. Children then were not witnessing family attending worship. Rather they began to see the hypocrisy in him. That has influenced how they are with their own families. It has caused problems in their marriages because of what they witnessed. It really discouraged one that was walking with the Lord, because of his father and other men in church being hypocrites it began to hinder his walk.

Me: Were you saved before you were married?

Louise: No.

Me: Do you feel that couples should be equally yoked?

Louise: Yes, because you want the saving knowledge of the entire household. If you are following Christ, you realize you need Christ to be head of the household. If you marry a saved person, it does not necessarily mean they will continue to follow Christ or grow spiritually either. But for us neither of us was saved at first so we were actually equally yoked in sin.

Me: Now that you are divorced, what are you looking for in a Christian counterpart?

Louise: A Christian man who you can really see Christ in, one that God really leads you to someone who is really saved. Where their lifestyle is one of prayer, consistency, and they follow the Word of God. I do not want a closet Christian where they are scared to admit it to folks and at work. I would like someone to exemplify on a daily basis that he truly lives it. Not their will but God's will be done in their lives. Not just someone that is tall, dark, and handsome, but what God brings me to complete me as a Christian. Having things in common to help complement each other in what we are doing.

Me: Do you have sex outside of being married?

Louise: No.

Me: What have you been saved from?

Louise: Sin. If you are not lining up with the Word, then it is sin.

Me: Do you invite people to church?

Louise: Yes.

Me: While you were married, did you flirt?

Louise: No.

Me: Did you ever have an affair while you were married?

Louise: No.

Me: What about any emotional affairs?

Louise: None.

Me: Did you hide things from your spouse during the marriage?

Louise: Yes, I did buy clothes and stick them under the bed, also money because of the situation in our marriage. I wish I could have been more open, but everything changed once he had backslidden. Everything became an argument.

Me: Do you watch or look at pornography?

Louise: No.

Me: Do you masturbate?

Louise: No.

Me: If you were on trial for being saved, would they have enough evidence to convict you of being saved?

Louise: Yes, I believe so.

Me: Do you think that people claiming to be Christians give Christianity as a whole a bad rap?

Louise: Yes, because you always hear that Christians are hypocrites.

Me: I really want to thank you for being open and honest.

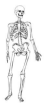

christian marriages defined by the world's ways

Are couples that pray together actually staying together? Or is prayer left out of the scenario all together? When tough decisions find you both, do you immediately go into prayer, turning it over to God for his guidance and answered prayer? Do you find yourself feeling at ease to pray with others more than your spouse? Maybe you find it less strenuous because you are not on one accord with your mate. Could it be that we are merely mimicking what we see the world do, which is just say grace together some of the time before dining and thinking that is enough?

Studies claim that Christians have a higher or just as high divorce rate as non-Christians. If so, do you find this to be alarming? What is the difference between our marriages and theirs? I understand that they divorce in the world for any reason, many because they feel they are not simply compatible. Let's look at the believer; have we tried praying, fasting, counseling, marriage retreats, basically anything short of ending the relationship?

Are the children growing up in loving atmospheres or one where one spouse is never around and all the bulk of the responsibility lies totally on you? You have to wonder if we are not truly committing our lives over to God in every area, then how are we going to commit to our spouses? As Paul talks about love in 1 Corinthians 13, we find that agape love, love that is unconditional at best. In verse 7 and just the beginning of verse 8 of that chapter it states, "bears all things, believes all things, hopes all things, endures all things. Love never fails" (1 Cor. 13:7–8, NKJV). Sure, when giving our love to someone, it may hurt and we perceive all the pain and shame that the situation has afforded us, but we should not stop trusting in God that he can be faithful to complete the work that he has begun in us or our spouses. I believe we should have enough faith in our Lord and Savior to see it come to fruition. If we give up to quickly, we will never truly know what God has ordained for us. The world is the one who lives in a microwaveable society not us I thought.

We must put the word into practice because it is not enough to attend service weekly and hear the word but never truly allow the word to take up root in our lives. "But be ye doers of the word, and not hearers only, deceiving your own selves" (James 1:22, KJV). Memorizing scriptures is not enough if we never apply them to our lives. First we must get into his Word and study it and, second, begin to walk it out and live it on a daily basis as we grow and mature in the things of God. It's like having a recipe passed down through generations, and you know that it had great success when people have followed it to a tee. Then you get your hands on it and decide to read it thoroughly till it clicked; now you are baking and you decide not to use the core ingredients because you think you know what to do and what you can substitute. Hours later it's done, and it does not even look like it should let alone taste the same.

In many situations, we must face the cold, hard facts that people do not love themselves nor have they been raised in the most loving and fostering environments. So for them they call this "normal chaos." We know that taking each other for granted is wrong, but we do it anyway. Like running a red light, we understand that we should not go through it—heck, it is the law—but someone explain to me why, time and time again why so many of us have done this at some time in our lives. We decide to leave our families long before the marriage is even over. This can be done when extramarital affairs begin to take place. Strongholds plague the very essence of our sense of responsibility, and we look around and think well everyone is having trouble so I am again just going to do what I recall seeing in my own home growing up or someone else's I know.

We have all heard the saying, "All men cheat." The question is how does society feel about men versus women cheating in general? The sad part of reality is that men being unfaithful to their spouses have been condoned by our society for years now. Society would likely enjoy patting them on the back and giving them cigars for all the notches they have on their bed posts. How refreshing it would be if we took a stand for what is morally right and explained to them how they are defiling themselves and their families. Women are frowned upon by society when they indulge in this same unfaithful act and are labeled to be promiscuous or a slut. I looked up the term "slut" on Wikipedia, and it defined it as, "Slut or slattern is a pejorative term meaning an individual who is sexually promiscuous. The term is generally applied to women and used as an insult or offensive term of disparagement, meaning 'dirty or slovenly.' It may also be used as an expression of pride in oneself or envy at the sexual successes of others."[2] The bottom line is that we all need to wake up and take off our rose colored specs and see that regardless of gender the act of cheating is sinfully wrong. Once again pose the question to yourselves—God's way or the world's way? "Thou shalt not commit adultery" (Exodus 20:14, KJV). This is not just a sin that we do against our mates, but more importantly we do this against God. Now if you have already participated in this act then its best to repent right now and get it right with God and your spouse.

"Husbands, love your wives, just as Christ also loved the church and gave himself for her" (Ephesians 5:25, NKJV). Husbands should live out what Christ has shown them in his love for the church. The church and Christ are one body, where it is meant that the husband and wife shall be of one flesh. How I treat my partner is really how I treat myself. So husbands, how are you treating your partners, or shall I say ultimately how are you treating yourselves? Are you treating your spouse as Christ treats his bride? Has Christ cursed or dogged the church out, disrespected it, cheated on it, or abused it when he felt the need?

Most things in life in order to grow need nourishment and to be cared for. We should love them as Christ even loves us and even pray that we will begin to see them as Christ sees us. Christ has a love for us that is full of grace and mercy; we cannot buy his love; we cannot force him to care for us even after we have sinned and fallen short of his glory. Yet and still he loves us, and he picks us up and dust us off and forgives us genuinely without holding an account of our wrongs. I wonder why is it that we continue to hold the other accountable even after we have forgiven them or maybe this is in the world and not something we Christians do in our own homes.

"Whoso findeth a wife findeth a good thing, and obtaineth favor of Jehovah" (Proverbs 18:22, ASV). Sounds like the wife that God provides to the man is in all actuality a blessing. Abba our father already knows the mate that he has for us. Not just going out and choosing anyone but seeking God in prayer for your mate and for his guidance and direction. Yes, it is the man finding the wife and not the other way around. Many women today feel that they want to take this responsibility on themselves. Why when God has already laid out the plan for us in his Word? That would suggest we have stepped out and again done something in similarity to the non-believer.

So many of our unions fall prey to the same characteristics of non-Christians. Many of our men have pride issues, and it can be easy for them to be with a group of men who are not saved, and they begin to call them henpecked or whipped. Now a man that is an unbeliever might take that to heart and feel it necessary to show his friends that he is still in total control. Somebody tell me why is it some of us take the same lowly road instead of rising above it and proclaiming and exhibiting godly love. We find ourselves coming home and putting our foot on our wives. Because we will not be punked out in public and made to feel inferior to any one, we must show them we wear the pants by hanging out with the guys very late and have a few brews or hit a blunt, none of the time calling the wife to inform her of our tardiness and plans. Simply put, because you are the man. How are we allowing our light to shine at that point? We are in the world but not of the world or has the lines become to blurry?

> Who can find a virtuous wife? For her worth is far above rubies. The heart of her husband safely trusts her; so he will have no lack of gain. She does him good and not evil all the days of her life.
> Proverbs 31:10–12, NKJV

Her moral character and integrity is far above rubies. A woman this godly can be hard to find, especially in this day and time because the world does not look at this as strength. A virtuous woman here in the text worked and also took care of her home and feared the Lord. Sounds to me as if this woman knew her worth. Many of us do not know our worth or even our worth in the Lord. A woman's attitude can change and win the heart of the husband.

> Likewise, ye wives, be in subjection to your own husbands; that, if any obey not the word, they also may without the word be won by the conversation of the wives; While they behold your chaste conversation coupled with fear. Whose adorning let it not be that outward adorning of plaiting the hair, and of wearing of gold, or of putting on of apparel; but let it be the hidden man of the heart, in that which is not corruptible, even the ornament of a meek and quiet spirit, which is in the sight of God of great price.
>
> 1 Peter 3:1–4, KJV

We must believe what God says about us and not what we see in videos depicting women to be merely sexual objects.

> For wives, this means submit to your husbands as to the Lord. For a husband is the head of his wife as Christ is the head of the church. He is the Savior of his body, the church. As the church submits to Christ, so you wives should submit to your husbands in everything.
>
> Ephesians 5:22–24, NLT

Many women feel like submitting is giving the husband permission to run all over them, and that is not what God means by submitting. This does not allow for the spouse to disrespect you in anyway shape or form. In Nelson's NKJV Study Bible it speaks of

> Just as Christ is not inferior to the Father, but is the second person in the trinity, so wives are equal to their own husbands. Yet in a marriage relationship, a husband and wife have different roles; to the Lord: A wife's voluntary submission arises out of her own submission to Christ.[3]

Then there are the emotional affairs that stack up against our character as well. We all know that more time is spent at work than home for the most part. There are so many kinds of office affairs that one can have, and not all are completely sexual or have not become that way yet. Two people of the opposite sex become intertwined with one another's lives. They enjoy each other's personalities in the work place and begin spending more and more time together. Now a portion of their day is spent conversing with each other, maybe lunch, at breaks, or after work before heading home. All too easily we begin sharing intimate details about ourselves, so when we arrive home sharing with our spouses is little to nonexistent, mainly because that need has been met.

Wikipedia defines an "emotional affair" as an affair, which excludes physical intimacy. It may also be called an affair of the heart. Where one partner is in a committed monogamous relationship, an emotional affair is a type of chase non-monogamy without consummation. When the affair breaches the agreement in the monogamous relationship of one of the partners to the affair, the term infidelity may be more apt.[4]

So as a saved person, what should we do differently? I personally feel this is a form of spiritual warfare. "The thief comes only to steal, and kill and destroy I came that you may have life and have it abundantly" (John 10:10, ESV). To uphold a marriage is the last thing on Satan's mind. He comes to us with something our sinful nature enjoys. I have looked at several Christian Web sites that have blogs and read that many claimed it was their prayer partner. Imagine going from one extreme to the next. That is just it though; if the enemy is allowed to control our thoughts day and night about someone other than our spouse, then he is winning the battle and not us. God is the difference between us and the world; he is able to restore the marriages we once knew to be lost. He can do more with our yes for full submission, so why are we not allowing him to do that work in us?

Yes, I said work, anything worth having is worth working at to maintain. That means putting the word back on the enemy. Proclaim what God says about you and your marriage. If you were getting caught up in something sinful, then stop and ask God for forgiveness and pray to him that you be delivered out of that trap. Then when it comes back, oh yes it will, shout out that you are no longer that person, for whom the sons sets free is free indeed.

We must know who we are individually first before we can even grasp who we are collectively later once we wed. Otherwise we will be spending all our resources and time searching for something or someone to fill us up. Like looking for love in all the wrong places. We will be looking tirelessly for the affection we cannot even give ourselves or replacing it with material satisfaction that—let's face it—never satisfies.

The world will tell us that we need a mate to complete us, just recall the movie *Jerry Maguire*. That is just one example in a world of many, where we have been made to feel as if we are lacking 50 percent of ourselves and until we find that someone who will then make us whole. With that in mind, we walk around with the assumption that we are not enough. I would rather know that my mate and I are 100 percent complete, and then when the two halves come together as one, then watch out world. Now we actually complement the other instead; where I am weak, then perhaps you are strong, and where your are quick to anger, I have more patience. Just more of a balance really, someone to bring out the best characteristics about yourself. Because if I were not complete and then I got married, everything I am and do is so caught up in that person that they become my god. I begin worshiping you for my mere creation, and I have now taken the focus off what is really important a relationship with my Lord and Savior. "Thou shalt have no other gods before me" (Exodus 20:3, KJV).

Communication is a key element in a marriage. Question is, do I communicate with you the way the world has engrained in my head or do I use the diagram in the Bible? He has already prepared a way for us to follow that works, strange how we deem it necessary to try everything else first. Most unions emulate what they saw growing up around them. No matter if we knew it to be wrong for many it is common place. In many of our childhoods, we witnessed one parent attending service regularly who was the saved one in the home, generally the mother. She would bring the word back to the husband who was not saved. Funny, when you ponder the thought that we can give you the word, but not take your test for you! That is what I call a moment of awakening.

We have seen firsthand disrespect, abuse, extramarital affairs, and in some cases an absent parent all together. This becomes what we practice in our own homes later on in life. There have been those that push everything up under the rug, which in turn we were unable to see an actual discussion of how things can be handled properly. We did, however, notice someone's blood pressure rising, anxiety attacks, and ultimately heart attacks because stress is a known killer when things become chaotic because they are not dealt with. Sort of like placing a ton of things into a miniature chocolate chest: one day the chest will burst open from all the baggage that has never been discarded of or resolved. At some point we have to be willing to face our problems head on and sit down as a family unit and work out the kinks. Not to say we will always agree but that we took the time to come to a solution together. Last I checked we were partners in this journey together.

Accountability and ownership kind of tie hand and hand. The term *accountability* is defined by Merriam-Webster as the quality of state of being accountable; especially: an obligation or willingness to accept responsibility or to account for one's actions.[5] This has been one major missing ingredient in many marriages. No one wants to be held liable for their own actions because we know with that comes consequences. Is it because many of us never saw anyone really take ownership of their mistakes, be it parents, pastors, or friends? Rather it is abuse, adultery, gambling, drugs, or alcoholism. We need to stand up and own what we have done and how it has impacted everyone around us. Too often we place the blame on the other person or people in our relationships. At the end of the day, wrong is wrong and right is right, so why allow false perceptions to be mirrored out in front of an audience? We should treat others like we would want to be treated, in fact even better. I say that because too often we think it is okay to lie to our mate because we think the truth hurts. It hurts more knowing that you have been deceived for a long period of time and that your mate kept you their other half in the dark with no regard to how that would make you feel. Look at the life of Christ and pray to God for strength in this area to be the examples we need in the earth.

The world's view of marriage is in part one without joy, sex, love, friendship, and commitment. We must keep in mind that God did not intend for it to be this way for the believer. Ask yourself whose route you are going to continue to travel down. I want all that God has purposed marriage to be, but I have to do my part for it to get there. I can't just sell it short for the fairy tales I have been told or the nightmares we see being worked out in divorce court either. It's like being dealt the hand we are given: do we make the best out of it or just settle for what is in front of us? In this microwave society, quitting is expected, so make up in your mind what type of marriage you want for yourself. One that is just simply not convenient or one that will give you beauty from the ashes.

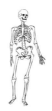

closet christians
or fake saints

If we do not confess him in public, can we truly serve him in private? If Christ were to come back in the flesh and show up as one of your co-workers for a season would he know you to be a Christian? This answer for many sadly would be no. Why would there be a need to keep Christ a secret in your life? Could it be because you would like your life to remain as normal so when you do something that goes against the word of God no one will be the wiser? So wait you accept Christ as your savior, never confess it, and then you wonder why things in your life seem to never get better. If I am going to be ineffective, why pretend on the Sundays that I do attend church services?

Perhaps this is the way the world lives on a day-to-day basis. Every day I wake up and put on my old self to please others because just think what they would say if they knew I had actually wanted or needed a fresh start. Maybe they would fire me, or I would lose business and then what would be left of me. My friends and family might even steer clear of me for the risk of me being different. Surely no one wants to hear me go on and on about how good God is. I know I am in the world, and I have to play by their rules. Instead of thinking how your change could be the very thing needed to evangelize to others. In many cases someone is waiting on you, your evolution to take place could ignite a fire that will blaze for all to see.

But instead we put on a mask to hide who we think we are becoming when in reality we are no more the wiser today then we were when we were unsaved. I am not telling you to announce it from the tops of buildings, even though that would be something to see or hear for that matter. Merely pointing out that when people notice that zeal you now have that they would in fact want it for themselves.

> That you may show yourselves to be blameless and guiltless, innocent and uncontaminated, children of God without blemish (faultless, unrebukable) in the midst of a crooked and wicked generation [spiritually perverted and perverse], among whom you are seen as bright lights (stars or beacons shining out clearly) in the [dark] world.
> Philippians 2:15, AMP

How can we win the world when our behavior and attitude exhibit the same characteristics as theirs? At some jobs it seems that using profanity has become increasingly popular like spewing jargon. Then of course it may look uncharacteristic of you when you decide to refrain from such tactics and people begin to see you as peculiar, and no one wants to hang out with you anymore because you are not considered to be down like the rest of them. If you are looking to please people more than God, how will you ever be a true Christian? You cannot serve two masters at once, the world and God. A choice needs to be made you will either follow Christ or man.

> You are the salt of the earth. But what good is salt if it has lost its flavor? Can you make it salty again? It will be thrown out and trampled underfoot as worthless. You are the light of the world—like a city on a hilltop that cannot be hidden. No one lights a lamp and then puts it under a basket. Instead, a lamp is placed on a stand, where it gives light to everyone in the house. In the same way, let your good deeds shine out for all to see, so that everyone will praise your heavenly Father.
>
> Matthew 5:13–16, NLT

How can we be salt and light if we keep our identity in him under wraps? It is not possible to affect change when we ourselves have not done so. When something is lacking flavor, we say it's bland. Are you a bland, saint? One definition of bland found in the Encarta World English Dictionary is: insipid, lacking flavor, character, or interest.[6] Being in Christ, our light will glow so that it cannot be hidden but there for the entire world to see. Many of us need to have our light relit since it burned out long ago.

The one place Satan does not want us showing up to is the workplace. He would prefer we take off our form of godliness long enough so that no one will be enlightened by it. So instead he wants us to get there and feel as if all hell is breaking loose and that we have nothing to shield us from the falling debris. The enemy would like nothing more than for our pressure to rise, and we hit a boiling point where are actions become more and more like theirs on a daily basis. At that point, imagine going to them trying to witness after you were the one that went on an outrageous rampage. Basically he wants to discredit you before you have that opportunity to change the atmosphere at hand.

This is one of those areas that if not defined brings us right back to living as the world does. Can you imagine if one of your coworkers were to visit your church unknowingly one day and see you up leading the praise team and you begin to flow in the spirit, what thoughts then would enter their mind about you? Do you think they would want what you have; they will instantly associate your behavior as hypocritical because they know who you are daily on the job and it is so far from this truth that they can only draw that one conclusion. At that point the enemy is thanking you because now this one may never step back into the house of the Lord again. Funny, I thought you were batting for the kingdom of God not of darkness.

In all actuality, this is what we do on an ongoing basis when we interact with others we have an awesome opportunity afforded to us if we choose to use it. It almost warrants the thoughts that you are ashamed.

> Therefore, everyone who acknowledges me be-
> fore men and confesses me [out of a state of one-
> ness with me], I will acknowledge him before my
> Father who is in heaven and confess [that I am
> abiding in] him. But whoever denies and disowns
> me before men, I also will deny and disown him
> before my Father Who is in heaven.
>
> Matthew 10:32–33, AMP

Now search yourselves and really ponder the thought of being denied or disowned before God. Well, could this be how he feels when you will not take the time out of your busy day to acknowledge him before men?

Is it fear that is stopping you from confessing to others around you of your relationship with Christ? The spirit of fear can keep you from moving forward in many areas of your life rather you believe it or not. "For God has not given us a spirit of fear, but of power and of love and of a sound mind" (2 Timothy 1:7, NKJV). In this day and time, many people are looking for something they can hold on to, some hope for tomorrow. What if God placed *you* deliberately on that job or that assignment to bring his word and his invitation to them and you decided not to? It could have been for that overly aggressive lady in the office that is always pushing her way on everyone else, and guess what she goes home night after night feeling so lowly and desperate and unloved. Then on this particular gloomy Monday, she decides it would be her last and she takes her life because it seemed as if no one cared. Do you really want that on your conscience knowing you were disobedient?

Many times we act as if we do not hear his voice telling us to invite someone to church or to just lend an encouraging word because we would prefer to just skip over that part. Fear, shame, and embarrassment can cause us to be unproductive saints. What is there to be embarrassed about in our country when in many areas of the world people are killed, beaten and sometimes ostracized because they claim Christianity? Would you say this is fair or simply their fault for acknowledging their faith out loud? The part that is astonishing is that they still proclaim Christ, no matter the circumstance or the punishment because they are walking in truth. What does that say about those of us who live in contrast to that very idea?

I read this next article (however not in its entirety) from the *Christian Post* by Aaron D. Taylor, a guest contributor wrote,

> Was U.S. Christian Slain in Muslim Mauritania 'Asking for It'?
>
> On Tuesday, June 23, 2009, an American Christian worker named Chris Leggett was gunned down by Al Qaeda for the alleged 'crime' of trying to convert Muslims to Christianity. To give you an idea of what kind of man Chris Leggett was, the 39-year old native of Cleveland, Tennessee, not only taught computer science in a low-class neighborhood in the capital city of Nouakchott, he also, according to the Cleveland Daily Banner, worked with the prison systems to train and equip women and young boys to re-enter society, directed a training center providing

training in computer skills, sewing, and literacy, and oversaw a micro-loan program which fostered the growth of hundreds of small businesses. Although the minuscule media coverage has been fairly straightforward, I was saddened to see some of the nasty comments on the Huffington Post when Ahmed Mohamed posted the Associated Press story on the site. Although a few of the comments unequivocally condemned Leggett's murder for what it is, a cowardly act of violence motivated by extremists, far too many seemed to think that Leggett was somehow 'asking for it' because of the nature of his work in a Muslim land, as if Chris Leggett somehow deserved to die because of his passion for sharing his faith. One commenter wrote, 'Well, you know, it is their country. You go walking around with arrogant disregard of their laws, you better be prepared to pay the consequences. Non-story.' Another commenter cut from the same cloth replied, 'I agree. It doesn't take much intelligence for non-military Americans to keep out of these countries. You not only go there at your own risk—you ask for it.' My beef isn't so much with the Huffington Post (who likely has little control over what people comment on the site), but to the people who made those nasty comments (there were some that were far worse), I would like to say to them: Feel free to criticize Christian missionaries working in Muslims lands, but I hope you realize that you're criticizing from a position of privilege. Many of you live in countries that allow you to choose your religious beliefs without fear of torture, imprisonment, or death. Hundreds of millions of Muslims live in countries that deny them that right. How do you know that out of the world's roughly 1.2 billion Muslims, that some of them don't want to hear another perspective? [7]

You have to wonder why in the so-called "free world" we are choosing to invoke a yoke of bondage around us willingly. When you compare the two, what is it that you come up with? Could it be that they have everything to lose and nothing to gain by publicizing who they have their faith in? So then what about you, those that reside on this liberated soil who have more freedoms awarded to them, why is it so hard to proclaim your love for God? Do not become like the Israelites who Jehovah set free but that wished they were still back in Egypt enslaved to the king. "Therefore if the Son makes you free, you shall be free indeed" (John 8:36, NKJV).

Maybe you feel you have a right to be embarrassed, for instance take a look at all the people claiming to be born again their lives are further from the truth. They are sometimes the ones with boldness speaking out and doing things that go against the very word of God and they are quick to use the title as "Christian" to link up their cause with their so-called faith. Do you feel that they are making a mockery out of your faith at this point? So then you decide that the best thing for you to do is steer clear of being associated or lumped into this wide spread arena. We have to really search ourselves to see if that is an all right response to such derogatory behavior.

Strong's Dictionary breaks down the word "Christian"; it's pronounced in the Greek as Christianos, which means follower of Christ.[8] In the Bible it states in Acts that it was first used as a word of contempt against the believers at Antioch. Prior to this they were called by different names: "brothers," "disciples," "believers," and followers of "the way" or "saints." The thought of being a genuine follower of Christ should be something that we all take seriously. Many have just taken the label and presented themselves as sheep in wolves clothing.

I came across a site where people were blogging and the title was "Ashamed to be a Christian." That was like a rude awakening; it displayed different people telling of their experiences with Christians and why they left the church as a whole. We should not allow a few bad apples to spoil the whole bunch. Stand up for what you believe in and hold true to your beliefs in God and do not be afraid to share your testimony with others in hopes of winning their souls. Stop living a life where people pleasing is all you do because the people in this world do not have a heaven or hell that they can place you in, but I know someone who does.

What if you were at heaven's gate and you figured, "Okay, Lord, I have been a good Christian, and now I want in." knowing good and well that you never took time to express to anyone your spirituality. For thirty years you kept it secret, and now you have gone on to be with your Lord and Savior. Only thing is that now you want Jesus to be a witness for you and tell God to let you in. Can you imagine if no one stood up for you and the sheer thought of not making it in became so real that you began to breathe erratically? Would you then wish you had taken time out of your busy day and just once told of his goodness? Or could it be that you feel his mercy and grace would be sufficient enough to just get you in? Honestly why wait till then ask yourself this now, and if you for one second feel that you would have this problem, then think how he feels when it's done to him.

sexual immorality still running rampant in the church today

Are there any of us that know the biblical views on sexual immorality, and if so, why are so many of us not yielding to it but instead following the characteristics supported by the views of this world? It is made quite clear in the Word how God feels about these sinful acts and how they are indeed punishable by death. Maybe you think that when you get to heaven on judgment day you will be able to persuade God to allow you to stay there and not send you into damnation for an eternity.

> So put to death the sinful, earthly things lurking within you. Have nothing to do with sexual immorality, impurity, lust, and evil desires. Don't be

greedy, for a greedy person is an idolater, worshipping the things of this world.

Colossians 3:5, NLT

When, if at all, are we going to wake up and declare that today is the day that we stop playing church and take to heart the seriousness of our actions? If you were to look inward and see what iniquities befall you on an everyday basis and actually begin to see how the lies you have even sold yourself are actually doing more harm than good by covering them up. Keeping them in a hidden state only allows the enemy free reign in your life because he is able to keep you in bondage in these areas. Let coming forth and walking in truth be the first step you take to shedding years of guilt and shame. Allow God to work through you and begin to see how your test will soon become your testimony. You are the only one holding you back, so cut your own umbilical cord to sin right now and begin enjoying your new life in Christ.

> Flee fornication. Every sin that a man doeth is without the body; but he that committeth fornication sinneth against his own body. What know ye not that your body is the temple of the Holy Ghost which is in you, which ye have of God, and ye are not your own? For ye are bought with a price: therefore glorify God in your body, and in your spirit, which are God's.
> 1 Corinthians 6:18–20, KJV

The dictionary meaning of the word found "fornication" means any unlawful sexual intercourse including adultery.

In the Bible the Greek definition of the word "fornication" means to commit illicit sexual intercourse.[9] Some types of fornication are adultery, premarital sex, pornography, homosexual acts, bestiality, and masturbation.

When most of us were younger, we really did not comprehend the importance of abstaining from sex before marriage. Grownups would always reiterate that it was not a good thing, but you never knew why. Now that I am married, I can see what the significance behind it would have meant for my marriage had my spouse and I actually reframed from it. Growing up in the church, we were taught right from wrong. Yes, we strayed away from the church and God when we figured out in our own minds that we wanted to partake in what everyone in the world was talking about. It was as if something had begun to spread over the airwaves and speaking for me. I felt like I had to experience it at some point because I was indeed in search of love but not the kind the Bible spoke of.

I had become like so many others where my light had burned out, and I felt like there was something so intoxicating about the savory smell of this new perfume that was being sprayed outside the church's doors. The world's views on sex before marriage are in contrast to that of the Word. Today in our society we see children younger and younger experimenting with sexual acts. I was a victim of rape in my late teens, and I began to be promiscuous soon after. I was in need of attention and had low self-esteem even though no one could tell. When I peered in the mirror, I saw something else looking back at me. What I saw staring back was a scared little girl who was so vulnerable and in fear of people leaving her. Coming from a home of divorce, I figured everyone leaves you sooner or later.

Not fully understanding or comprehending the fact that God alone had been there with me always throughout my years and that he was all I needed. Even when I rededicated my life back to him in my twenties, it was a struggle to abstain from sex all together. I would be celibate for so many months, and then there would be someone I was dating that agreed to the terms at first merely because of the animalistic challenge they saw before them. I had become their prey and they figured that after time they would seemingly tear down my resistance. In some situations they were able to because the sexual attraction I had for them had become more than I had originally anticipated for. Some would say they had a relationship with Christ because they figured that was exactly what I needed to hear.

Hearing the Word and actually applying it to our lives sit at extremely opposite ends of the spectrum. Instead we allow our flesh to get pleasure from people that were never destined to be our husbands or wives in the first place. We hop from one bed to another, and because the world has made it seem okay, we begin to practice by their rules and toss ours out the door, or shall I say put it in aside till we need it desperately. There are those of us who have shacked up together and no longer care about being married because the world says we need to know how a person is first before we marry them so that we will not regret it later. Down the road when we are married, thoughts enter our minds about some past sexual experiences or multiple ones that we shared with a soul tie. Now it's like we are in bed with everyone our partners and ourselves have had sexual intercourse with. Many of us, rather, we would be willing to admit it or not have begun sizing them up against our mates.

Now that leaves another door open with opportunities for us to want to reach out and touch someone if you catch my drift. Had we just stayed pure and been virgins, we would not know a touch of another other than the one we are united with. At that point we would not know if there was something better lurking around the corner because their body would be all we knew.

> So this I say and solemnly testify in [the name of] the Lord [as in his presence], that you must no longer live as the heathen (the Gentiles) do in their perverseness [in the folly, vanity, and emptiness of their souls and the futility] of their minds. Their moral understanding is darkened and their reasoning is beclouded. [They are] alienated (estranged, self-banished) from the life of God [with no share in it; this is] because of the ignorance (the want of knowledge and perception, the willful blindness) that is deep-seated in them, due to their hardness of heart [to the insensitiveness of their moral nature]. In their spiritual apathy they have become callous and past feeling and reckless and have abandoned themselves [a prey] to unbridled sensuality, eager and greedy to indulge in every form of impurity [that their depraved desires may suggest and demand]. But you did not so learn Christ!
>
> Ephesians 4:17–20, AMP

At what point are we going to start being real and stop playing by sitting up in church bleeding from the open wounds that are a direct impact of sin that we have allowed to cloud our judgment. Many of us have never seen a good example of people in ministry take a step down when they have slipped into this area of sexual immorality. Instead they go on hiding their illicit sins while their anointing ceases to exist. Would it not be refreshing for someone in leadership to take a stand and admit to falling and take a season to sit down and reflect while repenting and doing it with a sincere heart? Then allow God the time needed to make every crooked place in you straight by restoring you mind, body and soul. This could be the very thing that sets the oppressed flock among you free. We need to lead by example and trust God for our outcome.

Pornography is a huge issue that has swept through our pews and pulpits alike and people are generally none the wiser because of the mask its subscribers wear. The crippling affects are wide spread; from as early as childhood, to the breakdown of marriages, giving false realities of sex, the degrading affects on women, and of course it inhibits our relationship with God. It is self gratifying and it takes away the desire or affections towards a mate. It destroys trust and openness in a marriage relationship because it's often viewed in secret. Secrets as we know can lead to deception and lies which results in the other party feeling betrayed. Some possible signs of an addiction to porn are that it becomes a regular part of your everyday life. Also, problems in the bedroom will stem from this because you no longer find your mate alluring. Sleep patterns change because of the need to do this in private. Even wanting to act out what you have seen is a sign. Lastly keeping it as a secret habit because of the shame associated with it is yet another way of knowing. There are ways that a person who notices this behavior can be a positive influence. First you can start by becoming an accountability partner with them. Then suggesting they get in a support group where there are people there that have overcome or are dealing with the same addiction. It is defined by Wikipedia to be "the depiction of explicit sexual subject matter for the purposes of sexual excitement."[10] With the Internet now being another vehicle used to distribute this smut, the problem is ever increasing. Many cell users even have the World Wide Web on their phones now, so this can be viewed anywhere and at anytime without others suspecting a thing. *Forbes* did a column in 2001 that showed the industry's earnings between $2.6 billion to $3.9 billion. The breakdown had adult video at $500 million to $1.8 billion. The Internet at $1 billion, pay-per-view at $128 million, magazines at $1 billion.[11]

According to the statistics found on the Safe Families Web Site as of 2003, there were 1.3 million pornographic Web sites; 260 million pages. The total porn industry revenue for 2006: $13.3 billion in the United States; $97 billion worldwide. U.S. adult DVD/video rentals in 2005: almost 1 billion, and hotel viewership for adult films: 55 percent. Unique worldwide users visiting adult Web sites monthly: 72 million.[12] As you can see there was a significant increase in revenue from 2001 to 2006 and growing especially now adding in the cellular phone profits to this booming industry. The question is how much have Christians spent on this not only from a monetary standpoint but from the loss of their souls to this addiction?

> For you know what commandments we gave you by the authority of the Lord Jesus. For this is the will of God, your sanctification; that is, that you abstain from sexual immorality; that each of you know how to possess his own vessel in sanctification and honor, not in lustful passion, like the Gentiles who do not know God; and that no man transgress and defraud his brother in the matter because the Lord is the avenger in all these things, just as we also told you before and solemnly warned you. For God has not called us for the purpose of impurity, but in sanctification. So, he who rejects this is not rejecting man but the God who gives His Holy Spirit to you.
>
> 1 Thessalonians 4:2–8, NASB

At what point have we allowed the taste for sexual impurity to stop us from reverencing and being obedient to God? Is it so alluring that you are willing to miss out on eternity for moments of immediate pleasure?

Pornography is cited as a cause for the increasing divorce rates. What is really left when the spouse no longer views the intimacy in marriage to be beautiful as God intended it to be? Due to the perversion the world has sold us, most of us are not aware of its true meaning. In its raw graphic nature, it depicts that one mate can rarely fully satisfy that sexual appetite. Males are mostly aroused by images of a sexual content. Many were exposed to these images at early ages, maybe by finding the father's stash of dirty magazines or movies. So as a young boy, he was reared up to think of a woman as simply a sex object that was there to merely meet his sexual desire at that moment. Then by it being a hidden addiction where most of the wives are none the wiser, they felt that they had just been inducted into some secret society.

> But every person is tempted when he is drawn away, enticed and baited by his own evil desire (lust, passions). Then the evil desire, when it has conceived, gives birth to sin, and sin, when it is fully matured, brings forth death.
>
> James 1:14–15, AMP

The Mondofacto dictionary defines lust, which is "To have an eager, passionate, and especially an inordinate or sinful desire, as for the gratification of the sexual appetite or of covetousness; often with after."[13] I am not saying that sex is a bad thing, but I am stating that it needs to be in the confines of your marriage between you and your spouse (a man and a woman). It becomes difficult to act this out when something else is filling our thoughts every moment of the day. Thirsting and desiring to see another woman's or man's genitalia to bring you excitement dismantles the idea of your mate's body daily till one day it becomes almost impossible to get aroused by them unless you replace their face with another.

There is an old saying that has held true for years, what is done in the dark will eventually come to the light.

Your character can be defined by the activities you partake or indulge in when no one else is looking. The one thing we can be sure of is that God sees all and knows all and we can't hide who we really are from him. If you find it difficult to be proud and stand up in front of your spouses, children, parents, and pastors and proclaim that this has no effect on you, then be real with yourself. Next, be willing to acknowledge you need help ridding yourself of this habitual sin. Deliverance is mandatory if you truly never want to continue this lie and this lifestyle. Sure, the world may not have a problem with it, but ask yourself: does God? I really do not feel you will have to wait very long for that answer, and if the answer is like that of the world's, then I have to wonder who your God really is.

Pornography really places distrust and breaks down the bonds of unity in a marriage. Today there are an increasing number of women that like to look at different forms of pornographic material as well. I myself had to be delivered from this fleshly sin. There were days where I would not allow myself to be pleasured by my spouse simply because I had viewed x-rated movies earlier that day without my husband being the wiser. I was attending service regularly, and I felt I was a good Christian. Before I was saved and married, I would venture out to places that sold this kind of paraphernalia as if there was a rush even in that. Being a woman entering these establishments and purchasing what I felt I needed at that time was a big deal seeing as how they were more so frequented by men. I thought it was liberating the fact that I did not need a man to penetrate me to get sexual satisfaction.

Indeed that is how I began to look at it from there on out, so once I rededicated my life to Christ, this fleshly urge would come and try to overtake me. Sometimes I would just go to sleep and fight my sinful nature because I knew it was my dirty little secret, which only one other person knew about. Later on once I was married, I saw my spouse as simply someone to get me off because I was not sexually stimulated by him but really by lingering thoughts in my mind of porn stars I had became familiar with while I was out there in the world. I would envision myself being penetrated by them or some scene that was hot and steamy would flash before my eyes. For me that was easy because I had a photographic mind, and when they say a mind is a terrible thing to waste, I can testify to that truth. It might have been years, but I was able to go as far back as my father's old collection of sex tapes that I had found even as a child. Ones that I would look at again and again when I knew no one was home, those old VHS tapes and the stories in one of his magazines made me drift off into fantasy land because even at that time I was in love with descriptive story lines.

As young kids, my brother, cousins, and I would watch some of the movies together laughing as if we had this secret club. Little did we realize this was beginning to shape and cultivate our very minds of what actual sexual intimacy really was supposed to be between a man and a woman. It was something done for the most part outside the confines of a marriage; some involved orgies that depicted the need for more than one partner to truly feed your mounting sexual appetite. I had no problem with being married; it was now an issue of me needing my mate to arouse me sexually.

The same went for my husband; little did I know, we had been bitten by the same beast. He had his own small collection that I stumbled upon, and it made me livid. We were fighting the same spirit, not even knowing it. Mine where I dibbled and dabbled in the first two years, and his were more explicit. I had married myself, and now the reality of knowing that was why he was not finding me attractive anymore broke my heart. Not to mention it made my self-esteem tumble even lower than I knew humanly possible. I knew I did not look like any of the women he saw before him. I would throw his stash away only to find more in another spot weeks or months later. I recall going to him and spilling my beans about my own struggle that I was now learning how to rid myself of. I needed total accountability, and I was happy to be free in sharing this with him. He could not believe it—not me, his holier-than-thou wife. But you know what, it was me, and it made me take a cold, hard look at myself, and I was ashamed and carrying guilt, and I had to pray that God help me in this area and also to assist me with falling back in love with my spouse and finding him attractive all over again. I am thankful that with the help of the Lord I have been delivered and set free.

I believe that we cannot help anyone else in these areas unless we have been through them ourselves. This is an essential truth that shows you that if God can do it for me, he can do it for you as well. "Then Peter opened his mouth, and said, of a truth I perceive that God is no respecter of persons" (Acts 10:34, KJV). Many things we face in life are not entirely for us but for people that we may encounter on the journey. You may meet someone facing that exact obstacle later in life, and God places you with them for you to share your testimony in hopes of reaching them and letting them see that God can and will bring them out of bondage as well.

In many situations, we feel so ashamed that we fall away from God and the church as a whole. This is exactly what the enemy wants us to do so that we think our ties are now severed. Please do not buy this false reality we are able to ask God for his forgiveness and to help us in this area to be truly delivered. Instead we would prefer to be in the in crowd which is primarily the world. Most of us want to be seen as cool and no one wants to be labeled as odd or different. We have to remember that we are called to be set apart and to be peculiar people.

In the article "The Seduction of Pornography and the Integrity of Christian Marriage" by R. Albert Mohler, Jr., president the Southern Baptist Theological Seminary states that:

> The most important answer we can give to por-
> nography's rise in popularity is rooted in the
> Christian doctrine of sin. As sinners, we corrupt
> what God has perfectly designed for the good of
> his creatures and we have turned sex into a carnival
> of orgiastic pleasures. Not only have we severed
> sex from marriage, but as a society, we now look at
> marriage as an imposition, chastity as an embar-
> rassment, and sexual restraint as a psychological

hang-up. The doctrine of sin explains why we have exchanged the glory of God for Sigmund Freud's concept of polymorphous perversity.[14]

Wikipedia defines *polymorphous perversity* and gives us Freud's theory.

> Polymorphous perversity is as a psychoanalytical term for human ability to gain sexual gratification outside socially normative sexual behaviors. Sigmund Freud used this term to describe the normal sexual disposition of humans from infancy to about age five. Freud's theorized that humans are born with unfocused sexual libidinal drives, deriving sexual pleasure from any part of the body. The objects and modes of sexual satisfaction are multifarious, directed at every object that might provide pleasure. Polymorphous perverse sexuality continues from infancy through about age five, progressing through three distinct developmental stages: the oral stage, anal stage, and phallic stage. Only in subsequent developmental stages do children learn to constrain sexual drives to socially accepted norms, culminating in adult heterosexual behavior focused on the genitals and reproduction.[15]

Now in hearing this, I hope more people are aware of how they have belittled and demeaned the one flesh relationship.

While researching this topic, I found many alarming facts that broke it down where we could see how Christians alike are falling prey to pornography's clutches. Safe families Web site had "Christians, Pastors and Church Pornography Statistics and the Effects on Families and Marriages" which stated,

> A 1996 Promise Keepers survey at one of their stadium events revealed that over 50% of the men in attendance were involved with pornography within one week of attending the event. 51% of pastors say cyber-porn is a possible temptation. 37% say it is a current struggle. Over half of evangelical pastors admit viewing pornography last year. Roger Charman of Focus on the Family's Pastoral Ministries reports that approximately 20 percent of the calls received on their Pastoral Care Line are for help with issues such as pornography and compulsive sexual behavior. In a 2000 Christianity Today survey, 33% of clergy admitted to having visited a sexually explicit Web site. Of those who had visited a porn site, 53% had visited such sites "a few times" in the past year, and 18% visit sexually explicit sites between a couple of times a month and more than once a week. 29% of born again adults in the U.S. feel it is morally acceptable to view movies with explicit sexual behavior. 57% of pastors say that addiction to pornography is the most sexually damaging issue to their congregation. 47% of families said pornography is a problem in their home. The Internet was a significant factor in 2 out of 3 divorces.[16]

Pornography is a part of idolatry and can be something you worship and fixate on that begins to take the place of

God in your life. Paul discussed this in his letters to the Corinthian church in 1 Corinthians in dealing with their struggle with idolatry and immorality—the same things that are churches are dealing with today just in different ways. The same message is effective then and now, which is to stop trying to fit into the lifestyles of this world.

> Therefore let anyone who thinks he stands [who feels sure that he has a steadfast mind and is standing firm], take heed lest he fall [into sin]. For no temptation (no trial regarded as enticing to sin), [no matter how it comes or where it leads] has overtaken you and laid hold on you that is not common to man [that is, no temptation or trial has come to you that is beyond human resistance and that is not adjusted and adapted and belonging to human experience, and such as man can bear]. But God is faithful [to his Word and to his compassionate nature], and he [can be trusted] not to let you be tempted and tried and assayed beyond your ability and strength of resistance and power to endure, but with the temptation he will [always] also provide the way out (the means of escape to a landing place), that you may be capable and strong and powerful to bear up under it patiently.
>
> 1 Corinthians 10:12–13, AMP

This has become a global problem that has crossed borders, racial lines, and economic divides; and still we in the church are supposed to model Christ's behavior and conduct. Instead we are simply displaying a lack of self-control and discipline much like the rest of the world.

At what point are we going to be leaders in our communities and take a stand for what is morally repugnant and show the world there is a difference between us and them instead of always blending in? They are waiting on someone; will it be you? Will you allow God to reform your stinking thinking and make you an example for the masses to see? Ask God to truly come in and make you over today; right now, do not waste another minute being part of the problem when our Father in heaven has the solution already mapped out for you.

Having church as usual needs to come to a complete hault; we need to hear messages that deal with the issues at hand and see what God has to say about it instead of being scared that next Sunday the pews will not be filled. God is not concerned with numbers, especially when they are just taking up space and being allowed to stay comfortable in their sin. We must walk in love at all times, and in walking in love, we should not want anyone to go to hell because we cared more about how much the offering would be versus the count of souls saved and being delivered.

This is becoming more evident with the spirit of homosexuality in the church today, and yes, God loves the person but not the sin they are in. When we search the Bible to see if this is an acceptable lifestyle, what do we find?

> Don't you realize that those who do wrong will not inherit the Kingdom of God? Don't fool yourselves. Those who indulge in sexual sin, or who worship idols, or commit adultery, or are male prostitutes, or practice homosexuality, or are thieves, or greedy people, or drunkards, or are abu-

sive, or cheat people—none of these will inherit the Kingdom of God.

1 Corinthians 6:9–10 NLT

We cannot take sections from the Bible and say only these apply to our present-day society. Yes, we may feel that the times have changed, but to be honest, this was occurring back in biblical times with the cities of Sodom and Gomorrah. So is the Bible the same now as it was then? Yes, the message is the same, and no matter which way someone tries to change it to fit what they want it to be, it is wrong, and the cities were destroyed. "Jesus Christ the same yesterday, and today, and forever" (Hebrews 13:8, KJV). God's Word does not adjust to fit our ways, but we should transform to get in alignment with his word for our lives.

Many people feel that as long as they are attending church it does not matter if their sexual preference happens to be the same sex. Now it is one thing to lie to others, but really should we still be lying to ourselves? The Word clearly states we should not have sexual relations with the same sex. "You shall not lie with a male as with a woman. It is an abomination" (Leviticus 18:22, NKJV). *Abomination* in the Hebrew is *ba`ash*, which in Strong's #887 is to be a moral stench.[17] The definition in Encarta World English Dictionary says, "something horrible: an object of intense disapproval or dislike, something shameful: something that is immoral, disgusting, or shameful, intense dislike: a feeling of intense dislike or disapproval toward somebody or something (literary)."[18]

Sin separates us from God—any sin not just homosexuality. I believe God wants to deliver us all from our sinful nature. Flesh and spirit cannot dwell together; it has to be one or the other.

> There is therefore now no condemnation to them which are in Christ Jesus, who walk not after the flesh, but after the Spirit. For the law of the Spirit of life in Christ Jesus hath made me free from the law of sin and death. For what the law could not do, in that it was weak through the flesh, God sending his own Son in the likeness of sinful flesh, and for sin, condemned sin in the flesh: That the righteousness of the law might be fulfilled in us, who walk not after the flesh, but after the Spirit. For they that are after the flesh do mind the things of the flesh; but they that are after the Spirit the things of the Spirit. For to be carnally minded is death; but to be spiritually minded is life and peace. Because the carnal mind is enmity against God: for it is not subject to the law of God, neither indeed can be. So then they that are in the flesh cannot please God. But ye are not in the flesh, but in the Spirit, if so be that the Spirit of God dwell in you. Now if any man have not the Spirit of Christ, he is none of his. And if Christ be in you, the body is dead because of sin; but the Spirit is life because of righteousness. But if the Spirit of him that raised up Jesus from the dead dwell in you, he that raised up Christ from the dead shall also quicken your mortal bodies by his Spirit that dwelleth in you. Therefore, brethren, we are debtors, not to flesh, to live after the flesh. For if ye live after the flesh, ye shall die: but if ye through the

Spirit do mortify the deeds of the body, ye shall live.
For as many as are led by the Spirit of God, they are
the sons of God. For ye have not received the spirit
of bondage again to fear; but ye have received the
Spirit of adoption, whereby we cry, Abba, Father.

Romans 8:1–15, KJV

Then there are many on the DL (a.k.a. down low) and
in leadership capacities. I have a girlfriend that was married to an associate pastor, and for years he was leading a
double life and he only wanted to be intimate with her the
night before he gave a sermon. Believe me, he is not the
only one in church, in the pulpit, or in the gospel spotlight
that has hidden his sexuality. Today there is a number of
growing gay/lesbian churches as well. We are beginning
to resemble the very society we live in with no condemna-
tion. AIDS is becoming one of the number-one killers
for African-American women, and in this article "Why
AIDS is becoming a Black woman's disease and what we
can do about it—Health by Nikitta Foston," it states,

> Contributing to the alarming rate of infection are
> a variety of factors, including unprotected sex, sex
> with multiple partners, needle-sharing among in-
> travenous drug users, and the growing population
> of "down-low Brothers"—men who do not con-
> sider themselves gay or bisexual, but engage in sex
> with both men and women. The return of previ-
> ously incarcerated men into our communities also
> affects the rate of infection among Black women.
> "We have a huge population of African-American
> males who go into prison HIV-negative and come

out HIV-positive," says Thornton. "When these men get out, they come back to our daughters, our mothers and our sisters. They don't go back to men because they don't consider themselves gay."[19]

These disturbing facts are not something we should take lightly but truly make ourselves aware of and begin to pray for earnestly, just because it does not affect you currently does not mean that it is of less importance. While reading this next article that was in *The Guardian*/UK newspaper entitled "Black Women in US 23 Times as Likely to Get Aids Virus" by Gary Younge, I was moved to tears by our senseless demise. It states,

> African-American women are 23 times as likely to be infected with the Aids virus as white women and account for 71.8% of new HIV cases among women in 29 US states, government research shows. The principal theory as to why this affects women so acutely is because of the high rates of HIV infection among gay and bisexual men, which is six times that of whites and four times that of Hispanics, according to a 2001 CDC report. However, homophobia in the black community causes many men to live on "the down-low"— meaning they have public relationships with women and secret sex with men. A survey in Los Angeles county in 2001 found that 20% of HIV— positive African-American men said they had had sex with women in the past six months, compared with 9% of HIV—positive white men and 4% of infected Latino men." "Most women don't even

know they're at risk," said Cynthia Davis, an assistant professor at Charles R Drew University told the Los Angeles Times. "They find out when their spouse dies, or when they deliver a sick baby."[20]

Only God can deliver people out of this lifestyle; we cannot change anyone. And women thinking they can sleep with these men and magically change them is just foolish. Then for men who are not being upfront and honest know that your choices have extreme consequences that could not only harm you but harm innocent people to boot. The key here is that God is willing and waiting to forgive you and to truly deliver you out of your sin. We must come to him with a sincere heart and come knowing and believing that he alone is God and that you do not have to do this alone. God loves us and wants to cleanse us of all unrighteousness not because we deserve it but because of his mercy.

> He saved us, not because of the righteous things we had done, but because of his mercy. He washed away our sins, giving us a new birth and new life through the Holy Spirit.
>
> Titus 3:5, NLT

In many instances we are the only God people see in this world on a daily basis, and most of us, if not all, should stop and ask what God they see in us. Have they seen a God that is a deliverer, a healer, a way-maker or one who is useless in transforming us from our old selves and old lifestyles? If we are unable to believe him for these things, how can we go out and tell others to trust and follow him if there is no evidence of it in us? What is a test if we are unable to come out of it and produce a testimony worthy of his glory and praise and not our own? Staying knee deep in our sin is just that—we allow the light of God to weaken and dim. We want others to buy into a bill of goods that we are selling them that says, yes, he may be alpha and omega and he knows our end from our beginning, but the desires of my heart are too strong for me to allow God total and complete access to change that very thing I hold so dear because without it who am I really?

> Let no one say when he is tempted, "I am tempted by God"; for God cannot be tempted by evil, nor does he himself tempt anyone. But each one is tempted when he is drawn away by his own desires and enticed. Then, when desire has conceived, it gives birth to sin; and sin, when it is fully grown, brings forth death.
>
> James 1:13–15, NKJV

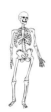

when it rains

When a turbulent storm takes place in your life, what are some of the ways that you handle it? Has your prayer life been built up in advance where you know that no matter what, you are going to lean unto God's unchanging hands? A lot is said for how we go into a storm, how we act during it, and especially the lesson learned or things changed when you come out. They say the best defense is really the best offense. Are you one that has run farther from God due to the tumultuous winds in your own life?

If we look at how the unsaved respond to adversities, what are some of the ways they handle their distress? Some commit suicide because things become too much for them to deal with. Others tend to go crazy, as if something just snapped from the inside out. There are those that need to build a false reality because bearing the enormity of the pain becomes too tough, so they turn to a temporary fix. This could mean drugs, alcohol, food, or sex, anything that will help them to escape their present state of mind. You have to wonder if we as believers are mirroring these same coping mechanisms.

Trials and tribulations were not designed to take you out of the race all together. We should be lifting up a standard in our lives that when they come—and yes, they will come—we know how to stand instead of fall away. Many times we only want to pray when things are chaotic because when things are going well, the sense of importance is no longer there. It could be that life is moving along without a hitch when suddenly everything goes belly up. Suddenly we are ill prepared for what is to come. In many facets, it is the same as going into battle without our ammunition. The battle is over before it starts because you have already surrendered in the enemies eyes.

There are some weapons we should be equipping ourselves with before the war even begins. Our praise and worship should not be something like good china, where we only break it out for special occasions. We should be doing this at home way before a crisis even comes our way. In our homes we should take the time to create an atmosphere one where we humble ourselves before God and worship him and praise him for his goodness. By doing this we can find fullness of joy in his presence.

> Make a joyful noise unto the Lord, all ye lands. Serve the Lord with gladness: come before his presence with singing. Know ye that the Lord he is God: it is he that hath made us, and not we ourselves; we are

his people, and the sheep of his pasture. Enter into his gates with thanksgiving, and into his courts with praise: be thankful unto him, and bless his name. For the Lord is good, his mercy is everlasting; and his truth endureth to all generations.

Psalm 100:1–5, KJV

The enemy is confused when he thinks that he has encamped all around you and you still have a "yet praise." We must give God praise no matter what it looks like because when we are down to nothing, that is when God is up to something. Praise is not conditional due to where we are, but it should propel us into our destiny. It will help you to take your mind off the situation and place it where it should have been all along on God. We should begin to praise him for what we already have. I am sure if we would just look around and take a mental inventory of what he has already blessed us with our outlook would begin to change immediately. The devil wants us to dwell on the problem instead of seeking God for the solution.

"I will bless the Lord at all times; his praise shall continually be in my mouth" (Psalm 34:1, NKJV). The definition of *praise* found in Webster is, especially, the joyful tribute of gratitude or homage rendered to the Divine Being; the act of glorifying or extolling the Creator; worship, particularly worship by song, distinction from prayer and other acts of worship; as, a service of praise.[21] So I am sure many wonder, *Why praise and why now, especially in these trying times?* This is exactly when we should be praising God because we believe he will turn it around.

Lots of us claim we want him to show up on our behalf, but we never fully trust him to do just that. We are so busy trying to figure it all out on our own that we take him out of the equation all together.

It should not take us being in a church to give God our best praise. Many of us that attend service weekly wait for the praise and worship team because we are looking to be entertained. After all God has done for us through the week, some if not most of us should be breaking the doors down praising God when we enter. Why is it that we can find reason to praise our favorite actors, singers, doctors, and lawyers but when it comes to the one who created all these people, we fall short in our praise to him? We can attend a concert and stand up at the right time and applaud when the entertainer comes out on stage and of course for an encore. Then there are the generous accolades that go to a doctor that just came out of surgery and tells you that someone you care deeply about is going to make it. When all along it has been God who has delivered you out of bondage, healed your body not once but many times over, won your case in a court where there was a gridlock, and woke you up every morning and granted you new mercies daily. Where is his praise? I suppose it went to someone else just like it has all along. Then we wonder why we find ourselves in the same predicaments and cannot seem to pull ourselves up and out of this vicious cycle.

> Because, although they knew God, they did not glorify him as God, nor were thankful, but became futile in their thoughts, and their foolish hearts

were darkened. Professing to be wise, they became fools, and changed the glory of the incorruptible God into an image made like corruptible man— and birds and four footed animals and creeping things. Therefore God also gave them up to uncleanness, in the lusts of their hearts, to dishonor their bodies among themselves, who exchanged the truth of God for the lie, and worshiped and served the creature rather than the Creator, who is blessed forever. Amen.

Romans 1:21–25, NKJV

Anytime the light goes off in us and we begin walking in darkness where we idolize people and things more than the one who created them, it's time that we need to check ourselves. Because at some point along the way we began to emulate the world and make graven images of man to be the gods we so dully serve on a daily basis. We did this by moving God out the way and placing man on the gold pedestals before us. Ask yourself where is God in that equation and if he would be happy with our results?

Worship, whether it's private or corporate, is a necessary component that will invite God's presence in. The Bible states that there is a particular way we should worship him; the question is: do we?

But the hour cometh, and now is, when the true worshippers shall worship the Father in spirit and in truth: for the Father seeketh such to worship him. God is a Spirit: and they that worship him must worship him in spirit and in truth.

John 4:23–24, KJV

Many of us want to worship him the way we see fit instead of the pure unadulterated truth. In many cases this becomes vain worship when it's not real and just for show or because your heart just is not in it and you are just doing this religiously as a ritual with nothing behind it.

> The Lord says: "These people come near to me with their mouth and honor me with their lips, but their hearts are far from me. Their worship of me is made up only of rules taught by me."
>
> Isaiah 29:13, NIV

During worship, one can be transcended; an open heaven can be above you where you can receive your breakthrough, your healing, and your deliverance. That is huge when you are faced with harsh circumstances and you have put your trust in God. You should take every occasion to begin worshiping him for who he is, what he has already done, and what he has yet to do in your life, instead of allowing the situation to get heavy and burdensome and begin to oppress you. If everything we do is in alignment to that of the world and they are watching to see our reactions when trouble comes, then we have not given them any reason to believe it's better over here.

Why not begin to go around your home and declare it holy ground and worship him there and just usher his presence in your home? Take time out to truly seek his face and be elevated to another level. There is no time limit attached to this; it should just be an outpour that is real and honest. I will sometimes put a CD in that has worship songs on there, and I will begin to create an atmosphere for worship. Other times I may even sing a song myself that just lets him know I need him. Allow the Holy Spirit to take over as you rest in his presence. You can wait till Sunday if you want while going through hell all week long, or you can begin to get before him now and see him transform it. To get a different result sometimes we have to be willing to do a new thing.

Having a true prayer life and even prayer partners are vital in this journey. Knowing that you are free to go to God in prayer and make your request known and believing that it will be answered should give you a sense of solace knowing God is working on your behalf. Prayer can change things around; it can bring you the peace within and joy abounding in your heart—joy that the world did not give you nor should be able to take from you. Even some non-saints will call on God if pressed hard enough against a wall after they have tried everything; then how much more should we be able to call on the name of Jesus? I thought we were the ones that had the *real* relationship with him.

In true worship we are submitting to God's will and turning ours over. But let me be clear; this does not mean giving it to him in worship then after going back to your own will for your life. At some point we should know that God has our best interest at heart. His plans for us far outweigh what we could ever concoct for ourselves. Many of us have tried bargaining with God and making deals then once we get our way it's like "Okay, Lord, I do not need you to steer the wheel anymore." If we were doing such a great job with it, then why did we need him to take it in the first place?

Prayer is a powerful weapon when we are combating the tricks of the enemy. Having a prayer life is crucial in this daily walk, knowing that we can take every care and concern to our Father in heaven and leaving it there is cathartic.

> Casting the whole of your care [all your anxieties, all your worries, all your concerns, once and for all] on him, for he cares for you affectionately and cares about you watchfully.
>
> 1 Peter 5:7, AMP

The enemy would want nothing more than for us to go through our lives defeated and depressed like many people in the world today. I can attest that it gets rough sometimes and we have to pull ourselves up and remember that our joy, which is from the Lord, is not dependent on our mood. God is the source of our joy, and when we really get the knowledge of that on the inside of us, we can pray knowing that Jehovah will meet the needs of his people.

Understand that there is nothing too hard for our God; what seems impossible to us is possible with him. This should give us a sense of boldness when we go to the throne that we can speak those things that be not into existence.

> As it is written, "I have made you a father of many nations" in the presence of Him who he believed—God, who gives life to the dead and calls those things which do not exist as though they did.
>
> Romans 4:17, NKJV

Many of us have not because we ask not. I recall my father always saying, "Closed mouths do not get fed." We could apply the same rule of thumb here.

We have the power to speak to our mountains and have them be removed. Are you believing God for something in your life right now that you want to be rid of? Then begin speaking the Word of God in prayer back to him because his Word will not return void to you unlike that of man.

> For assuredly, I say to you, whoever says to this mountain, "Be removed and be cast into the sea," and does not doubt in his heart, but believes that those things he says will be done, he will have whatever he says.
>
> Mark 11:23, NKJV

Now when you pray, you must believe that it is done, or you have just basically wasted your time.

It's time we take back what the enemy has stolen from us, our families, marriages, children, jobs, homes, and vehicles. Stand up in prayer and profess that he will no longer rob you of everything that it stops today. Put the devil under your feet, begin to declare that your home is holy ground, and declare that your husband or wife is coming back if you two are separated. With authority declare that your children are saved, that they will no longer be drug addicts. Tell the enemy *no* and that you will no longer be quiet and dismissive that the God in you is ready to fight. Take it back, get a prayer partner, and believe that there is power in two or more people standing in agreement together.

> Truly, I say to you, whatever you bind on earth
> shall be bound in heaven, and whatever you loose
> on earth shall be loosed in heaven. Again I say to
> you, if two of you agree on earth about anything
> they ask, it will be done for them by my Father in
> heaven. For where two or three are gathered in my
> name, there am I among them.
>
> Matthew 18:18–20, ESV

Prayer allows us the opportunity to commune with God, if we are constantly in prayer believing God and standing on the word, then when trials and tribulations enter the picture we should have a firmer ground on the whole situation. The wind should not be able to just come in and blow your house down if it was built on a solid foundation to begin with. Prayer needs to be our first form of attack; sadly enough, it has become a last resort for many of us. Too often we act just as defenseless as the rest of this world. Without prayer we reside in a constant state of chaos and confusion. Stop going through life not knowing which side is up, always waiting on the other shoe to just drop down in front of you.

That is why studying and getting clarity of the Word are so crucial in our everyday walk. It gives us basic instructions for this spiritual war we are in.

> Put on the whole armor of God that you may be
> able to stand against the wiles of the devil. For we
> do not wrestle against flesh and blood, but against
> principalities, against powers, against the rulers
> of the darkness of this age, against spiritual host

of wickedness in the heavenly places. Therefore take up the whole armor of God that you may be able to withstand in the evil day, and having done all, to stand. Stand therefore, having girded your waist with truth, having put on the breastplate of righteousness, and having shod your feet with the preparation of the gospel of peace; above all, taking the shield of faith with which you will be able to quench all the fiery darts of the wicked one. And take the helmet of salvation, and the sword of the Spirit, which is the word of God; praying always with all prayer and supplication in the Spirit, being watchful to this end with all perseverance and supplication for all the saints.

Ephesians 6:11–18, NKJV

The Word is the sword of the Spirit, and it's to be our weapon of choice in defending ourselves against the tricks of the enemy. When the devil brings thoughts to our minds that come to tear you down, we are to speak what the Word says about us back to the enemy to get him to flee. Buying his lies are no longer an option because the God that lives in us says we have the victory. Our battle is in the spirit world with the unseen evils of this world. The Word is alive and very powerful, and all we need to do is open our mouths and begin professing it.

For instance, in the physical we have an immune system that fights against diseases and sicknesses that come to do harm to our bodies. Then we have the military that defends the US soil when threatened of an attack. Someone tell me why as Christians we sit idly by allowing destruction and mayhem around us and still we do nothing. We are not useless; just look at the best example given to us by Jesus in Matthew chapter 4.

> Then Jesus was led up by the Spirit into the wilderness to be tempted by the devil. And when he had fasted forty days and forty nights, afterward he was hungry. Now when the tempter came to him, he said, "If you are the Son of God, command that these stones become bread." But he answered and said, "It is written, Man shall not live by bread alone, but by every word that proceeds from the mouth of God." Then the devil took him up into the holy city, set him on the pinnacle of the temple, and said to him, "If you are the Son of God, throw yourself down. For it is written: he shall give his angels charge over you, and, in their hands they shall bear you up, lest you dash your foot against a stone." Jesus said to him, "It is written again, you shall not tempt the LORD your God." Again, the devil took him up on an exceedingly high mountain, and showed him all the kingdoms of the world and their glory. And he said to him, "All these things I will give you if you will fall down and worship me." Then Jesus said to him, "Away with you, Satan! For it is written, you shall worship the LORD your God, and him only you shall serve." Then the devil left him, and behold, angels came and ministered to him.
>
> Matthew 4:1–11, NKJV

Let us take a look at some of the weapons they used in the biblical days with certain warriors that joined David's army. In 1 Chronicles 12 it talks about the ones who used slings, bow and arrows, shields and spears—all experts in using their weaponry in times of battle. They spoke of their strength and agility. It was said that David had a great army of soldiers. What was so special about these men and how had they become such great fighters? Mainly due to their skillfulness which for all practicing long and hard speaks volumes. I am sure that they had to be mentally prepared as well for combat. We should be the same in this spiritual battle we are in by having our minds stayed on the Word of God so we can face encounters head on.

Sometimes it is necessary to pull away from everything this includes the television, computer, and telephone. Get into a place where you can study your Bible and begin memorizing scriptures. "Be diligent to present yourself approved to God, a worker who does not need to be ashamed, rightly dividing the word of truth" (2 Timothy 2:15, NKJV). Why is studying the Word such a hard task for us? Is it that we have no real interest in learning the Word daily because we can listen to our pastor during service and then just repeat what they said if someone were to ask us? Think about it: most times when the enemy attacks, we are alone and it's not like we can tell him to hold on, let us get the pastor on the phone so that he can give him a word to make him flee. We must be well prepared and equipped for battle, and there is no better way than familiarizing ourselves with God's Word.

If we were to go into most people's homes we would find a Bible somewhere stashed inside, maybe even out for show so that visitors can conclude that we feast from it often enough.

Even hotels have them in the drawer of the nightstands so that you can read them in your spare time. Once again the question comes to mind: how many of us really take time out to learn the Word? Could the answer be that we put it on a shelf till disaster strikes, then that is when we take it down and dust it off in hopes that we can find an answer. This for some could become a time of desperation because your turn around time needs to be now and we begin to get discouraged because of a lack of preparation.

There were many references in the Bible that showed how people were healed because of their faith, which is described in the word as now faith. "Now faith is the substance of things hoped for, the evidence of things not seen" (Hebrews 11:1, KJV). Faith is defined as belief and trust in and loyalty to God: belief in the traditional doctrines of a religion: firm belief in something for which there is no proof: complete trust. Some of us can put complete and utter trust in man but fall short when it comes to our Heavenly Father. Then we are surprised when man lets us down time and again. We must believe that through it all God will deliver us out of the pit we are in. You will not get very far if you only go through the motions without fully trusting in God to turn things around for you.

Putting all our faith in God to deliver us from the snare of the fowler or the trap of the enemy is a call to action. We can pray, praise, worship, and speak the Word, but without faith it's useless. Faith will take it to the next level; it will show that our belief is so strong in God that it may look bleak to others but to us it's an opportunity for God to do a miracle.

Do not, therefore, fling away your fearless confidence, for it carries a great and glorious compensation of reward. For you have need of steadfast patience and endurance, so that you may perform and fully accomplish the will of God, and thus receive and carry away [and enjoy to the full] what is promised. For still a little while (a very little while), and the Coming One will come and he will not delay. But the just shall live by faith [My righteous servant shall live by his conviction respecting man's relationship to God and divine things, and holy fervor born of faith and conjoined with it]; and if he draws back and shrinks in fear, My soul has no delight or pleasure in him.

Hebrews 10:35–38, AMP

Some of us allow our faith to waiver depending on how long we have been waiting on an answer. We must allow patience to work in us during these times, especially because we could be hours or days away from our breakthrough and allow doubt to seep in and begin speaking negatively over the situation.

I waited patiently for the Lord; And He inclined to me and heard my cry. He brought me up out of the pit of destruction, out of the miry clay, And He set my feet upon a rock making my footsteps firm. He put a new song in my mouth, a song of praise to our God; many will see and fear and will trust in the Lord.

Psalm 40:1–3, NASB

Having faith is having full confidence that God cares for us and our needs. In the natural we often want to call up our friends or members of our family and tell them all our problems, and for the most part, they cannot help you out at all. What if we tried calling God up and telling him exactly what is going on in our lives; do you not believe that he will do even more than just listen?

> Don't worry about anything; instead, pray about everything. Tell God what you need, and thank him for all he has done. Then you will experience God's peace, which exceeds anything we can understand. His peace will guard your hearts and minds as you live in Christ Jesus.
>
> Philippians 4:6–7, NLT

What is it the world puts its trust in on a daily basis, and how does that work for them? Many people put their faith in objects; they have good luck charms that do not amount to a hill of beans. You have thousands if not millions of people who rely on winning the lottery even though their chances are slim. There are those that contact a physic friend or a spiritual advisor, as they call it today, to help them down a particular path. Others place their belief in material gain; they look to what they have and how that makes them feel as a person. Some even keep theirs embedded in stocks and bonds, and then when that crashes, what is left of their security then? It comes down to what makes individuals feel secure: people, places, and things.

Our faith as Christians should be like that of Abraham when God told him that he would be a father of many nations. We should have a strong sense of hope in spite of what it appears to already be in the natural.

> Who against hope believed in hope, that he might become the father of many nations, according to that which was spoken, so shall thy seed be. And being not weak in faith, he considered not his own body now dead, when he was about an hundred years old, neither yet the deadness of Sarah's womb: He staggered not at the promise of God through unbelief; but was strong in faith, giving glory to God; And being fully persuaded that, what he had promised, he was able also to perform.
>
> Romans 4:18–21, KJV

It is time to place your faith in the one person who we know will bring it to pass for us.

How many times have you sat down and made out plans for your life and they never to seem to work out quite like you planned? Or maybe you got exactly what you wanted and still you feel empty and if there is something missing. That something is God; he has a great plan for your life if you would just step out on faith and trust him with it.

> We do this by keeping our eyes on Jesus, the champion who initiates and perfects our faith. Because of the joy awaiting him, he endured the cross, disregarding its shame. Now he is seated in the place of honor beside God's throne.
>
> Hebrews 12:2, NLT

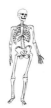

life after death

The Bible is very vivid as it details the consequence of sin once we begin to let it seep into the crevices of our minds where it becomes a habitual lifestyle. After time it becomes like a debilitating and crippling disease. It results in a spiritual death, which is a separation that takes place between God and ourselves.

> Their moral understanding is darkened and their reasoning is beclouded. [They are] alienated (estranged, self-banished) from the life of God [with no share in it; this is] because of the ignorance (the want of knowledge and perception, the willful blindness) that is deep-seated in them, due to their hardness of heart [to the insensitiveness of their moral nature].
>
> Ephesians 4:18, AMP

God can still grant you another opportunity even after a spiritual death has occurred. This happened to the Israelites in the book of Ezekiel as well. Due to the idolatry, sexual immorality, and their love of sin they had to become dead before a spiritual rebirth could take place. There are plenty of similarities between the nation at that time and our nation now. Today we take God's love toward us for granted as well. We too have become like the adulterous wife just as Jerusalem had done so many years ago. God no longer has first priority in our lives; instead he has taken a back seat to everything else on a day to day basis. We have traded our time with God and sold it out for the lust of our flesh, which to us holds a higher degree of importance. This great nation of ours has become so chaotic because over a period of time we have slowly taken God out of everything including government, schools, and more importantly ourselves. The society we live in is one of mixed up morals and self-indulgence where it seems that anything goes.

All throughout the Word from Genesis to Revelations there has been a messenger that was handpicked by the Father to deliver a message to a lost people. In every situation, there was a warning but was too often ignored or overlooked. We are not victims of the times, but instead we have become a major component symbolizing the very essence of what went wrong. Too often we assume to know more than God and the assumption goes on from there and trickles down to the Bible where we begin to think of it as an archaic source no longer prevalent in modern times. As if the choices we make have no lasting effects because if we can disqualify the source then there is no need to live by its standards.

What is life as we know it is just a passing frenzy where we hop and jump from one fad to another without rhyme or reason? Or is life to be cherished and the time we have been blessed with a gift that we unwrap daily where the impossibility of the moments added up equal's mere grace. Whose dreams are you chasing: the ones embedded down on the inside or the ones that society has told you are of critical importance? In many cases, I believe we choose to forget and then measure our successes by the world's standards and then feel depressed when in their eyes we seem to have fallen short. In reality it is mainly because we pursued things that never were intended for us to begin with, when the only thing that really counts is how God sees us and where we place on his scale.

It is time we take an inventory of how the love of sin can push us right out of the will of God where the mere nutrients that keep us alive are no longer at our disposal. Every year we sit down and make New Year's resolutions by seeing what needs to be different in our lives with this coming year. Many of us first opt to lose weight because we over indulged during the holiday festivities. Then there are the ones who say they are going to stop smoking, quit drinking soda, read more, get back in school, become debt free, find a mate, and some even declare they will find a new career. While reading that list, there was nothing on there that focused on getting a deeper relationship with Christ. We rarely see "pray more" or "find a church home" if we are without one at the time. All the things that were listed can be accomplished by putting God first but instead we opt to do it alone. I believe that so many of us give up on the resolutions because it's difficult to do those things without support or someone guiding and directing our paths. We have to ask ourselves why Jehovah is continually left off our list.

Many of us today will follow a false teacher or prophet because we only want to hear something that soothes our egos. The truth cuts too harshly, so instead we would prefer to listen to the lies of the enemy and buy into it because at the end of the day it should be all about us and our wants anyway. On a daily basis, it becomes easier and easier to take God out of the scenario all together. We have to acknowledge what it is we have placed more emphasis on than God. For many of us, what we idolize takes precedence over our maker where we begin to worship people and things more than we do God.

The Israelites were caught up in worshiping sexual misconduct, sorcery, spiritism, snake worship, child sacrifice, and in worshiping idols in high places. Let us take a closer look at what we give reverence to more than that of our father in heaven. First we have money for many this is the crème de la crème; we would do almost anything to have it. "For the love of money is a root of all kinds of evil. Some people, eager for money, have wandered from the faith and pierced themselves with many griefs" (1 Timothy 6:10, NIV). There are many of us who literally love—and I mean *love*—money and let us not forget what money can afford us that most people are really thriving after.

That brings us to material gain, which society looks differently at the haves versus the have nots. So for a lot of people, it is important to possess things; it does not matter if at the end of the day we go broke, as long as we have a house full of material to keep us warm at night. Sometimes we can look up and we have all this stuff and no one to share it with, because in reality it was more important attaining these things than actually putting stock into anything else. Our fantasy is to live like the rich and famous, which brings us to fame. This is what we see played out on the big and small screen people going from rags to riches. Then to top it off, many of them become famous at young ages. Now they are on television showing us their cribs and their whips, and this strikes a chord in us because we have not accomplished anything near. In turn it begins to make us feel bad about ourselves. Something else we notice is that they say they acquired this God-given talent on their own.

To break this down in laymen's terms, they elected to throw God away; this to us becomes alluring because we too want fame and fortune. We begin to work their formula into our lives and center on Christ less and less till one day he is out of the picture all together. Some of us heard that our favorite rappers were once thugs that hustled for a living, and that hustling mentality is what worked in their favor. Now we are thinking of quick get-rich schemes because if it worked for them, shucks, we know it can work for us. Little did we know that selling our souls would come at such a greater cost; but in that moment, it all seems worthwhile.

Then if we look at the Christians that are famous and they tell their story and we hear that for years they labored to get to this point and that they had to become broken in the process. That word *broken* is not the most alluring term, so needless to say, we turn away from their struggle all together. Because what we heard is that this was a process, one that cost friends, even family members turned their backs on us. Who wants to go through life alone and as a cast away? Not many. I gather that is why they say ignorance is bliss, because "without man" does not mean that you are alone. It simply means that God is with you and that he has just separated you for a season to transform your life.

The people of Jerusalem did not want to break their alliances either; they had become like a poor man's prostitute in that they got nothing out of the deal but gave away their treasures foolishly.

> Son of man, confront Jerusalem with her detestable sins. Give her this message from the Sovereign Lord: You are nothing but a Canaanite! Your father was an Amorite and your mother a Hittite. On the day you were born, no one cared about you. Your umbilical cord was not cut, and you were never washed, rubbed with salt, and wrapped in cloth. No one had the slightest interest in you; no one pitied you or cared for you. On the day you were born, you were unwanted, dumped in a field and left to die. But I came by and saw you there, helplessly kicking about in your own blood. As you lay there, I said, Live! And I helped you to thrive like a plant in the field. You grew up

and became a beautiful jewel. Your breasts became full, and your body hair grew, but you were still naked. And when I passed by again, I saw that you were old enough for love. So I wrapped my cloak around you to cover your nakedness and declared my marriage vows. I made a covenant with you, says the Sovereign Lord, and you became mine. Then I bathed you and washed off your blood, and I rubbed fragrant oils into your skin. I gave you expensive clothing of fine linen and silk, beautifully embroidered, and sandals made of fine goatskin leather. I gave you lovely jewelry, bracelets, beautiful necklaces, a ring for your nose, earrings for your ears, and a lovely crown for your head. And so you were adorned with gold and silver. Your clothes were made of fine linen and were beautifully embroidered. You ate the finest foods—choice flour, honey, and olive oil—and became more beautiful than ever. You looked like a queen, and so you were! Your fame soon spread throughout the world because of your beauty. I dressed you in my splendor and perfected your beauty, says the Sovereign Lord. But you thought your fame and beauty were your own. So you gave yourself as a prostitute to every man who came along. Your beauty was theirs for the asking. You used the lovely things I gave you to make shrines for idols, where you played the prostitute. Unbelievable! How could such a thing ever happen? You took the very jewels and gold and silver ornaments I had given you and made statues of men and worshiped them. This is adultery against me! You used the beautifully embroidered clothes I gave you to dress your idols. Then you used my special oil and my license to worship them. Imagine it! You set before them as a sacrifice the choice flour, olive oil, and honey I had given you, says the Sovereign Lord. Then you took your sons and daughters—the children you had borne to me—and sacrificed them to your gods. Was your prostitution not enough? Must you also slaughter my children by sacrificing them to idols? In all your years of adultery and detestable sin, you have not once remembered the days long ago when you lay naked in a field, kicking about in your own blood. What a sick heart you have, says the Sovereign Lord, to do such things as these, acting like a shameless prostitute. You build your pagan shrines on every street corner and your altars to idols in every square. In fact, you have been worse than a prostitute, so eager for sin that you have not even demanded payment. Yes, you are an adulterous wife who takes in strangers instead of your own husband. Prostitutes charge for their services—but not you! You give gifts to your lovers, bribing them to come and have sex with you. So you are the opposite of other prostitutes. You pay your lovers instead of their paying you!

Ezekiel 16:1–34, NLT

Reading those scriptures, you feel that Jerusalem was wrong, but ask yourselves, have we not done the same thing or even worse to God ourselves? After all he has done for you, we still ignore him and place more emphasis on worldly pleasures and selfish gain. This world has turned its back on God again and again; the worst part is that most of those that have done this still carry the title "Christian." God sent his son as our savior to redeem us back to him, and yet we still treat him as obsolete. Even after he picked us up and dusted us off and washed us in the blood.

The Spirit of God has not visited many churches today, but we still function as normal. How can this be when there is no real anointing taking place? We are in the pews, some churches fuller than others, yet if we look closely, we can see dead images of our former selves acting out a service rather than actually being alive in it. Quit buying into the notion that you have the best of both worlds when the truth is the sale of your soul to the devil is ever present. Are you not tired of having less than God's best in your life? Why continue to walk around in a lifeless decomposed state when there is a restorer out there? When are you going to stop claiming to be adopted into a family for namesake only when you could be partaking in the fullness of its privileges?

We have become spiritually dead like the valley of dry bones. Our life support has been cut off from its supply, and yet we are still parading around as if we are connected. Is living and dying in sin more important than serving the Father? Just like then, God is still saying that there is life after death. Come out of captivity and allow him to begin a new work in you and to awaken the spirit inside. God has not given up on you; why give up on yourself? Reach out to the one that can make it right within your entire being and be the person you were destined to be.

The hand of the Lord was upon me, and he brought me out in the Spirit of the Lord and set

me down in the midst of the valley; and it was
full of bones. And he caused me to pass round
about among them, and behold, there were very
man [human bones] in the open valley or plain,
and behold, they were very dry. And he said to
me, Son of man, can these bones live? And I answered, O Lord God, You know! Again he said to
me, Prophesy to these bones and say to them, O
you dry bones, hear the word of the Lord. Thus
says the Lord God to these bones: Behold, I will
cause breath and spirit to enter you, and you shall
live; And I will lay sinews upon you and bring up
flesh upon you and cover you with skin, and I will
put breath and spirit in you, and you [dry bones]
shall live; and you shall know, understand, and
realize that I am the Lord [the Sovereign Ruler,
Who calls forth loyalty and obedient service]. So I
prophesied as I was commanded; and as I prophesied, there was a [thundering] noise and behold,
a shaking and trembling and a rattling, and the
bones came together, bone to its bone. And I
looked and behold, there were sinews upon [the
bones] and flesh came upon them and skin cov-
ered them over, but there was no breath or spirit in
them. Then said he to me, Prophesy to the breath
and spirit, son of man, and say to the breath and
spirit, thus says the Lord God: Come from the
four winds, O breath and spirit, and breathe upon
these slain that they may live. So I prophesied as
he commanded me, and the breath and spirit came
into [the bones], and they lived and stood up upon
their feet, an exceedingly great host.

Ezekiel 37:1–10, AMP

God wants to breathe new life into your hollowed existence and resurrect your frail body from the ruins. If you are reading this and it has pierced your soul, know that he is waiting with outstretched loving arms for you right now. Today is your day; it is not too late; do not allow another missed opportunity to pass you on by. Time is of great importance; start refocusing yours in the right direction, which will help spring forth the right attitude. It does not matter if man says no because our Father in heaven says yes to your new beginning.

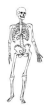

epilogue

I often listen to successful people and they tell you how much time they put into their work. When you think about it, they were practicing their craft, and they say practice makes perfect. So anything you work at in life and give your all in, you can accomplish and learn from your mistakes on the way. How can you live a holy life if you are not even willing to put your best foot forward? Study your Word daily, meditate on the Scriptures, begin setting aside a time for prayer, and begin to build a personal relationship with God. Begin walking upright, putting one foot in front of the other one at a time, and petitioning the Father for strength in this journey.

How is it possible to reap the fruit of your labor if you are not willing to work at something? You have to try God at his Word, test it, and watch it come to pass. God can do all things but fail. There is no blessing without a battle. Many days you may feel like giving up, because you have hit a bump in the road. Remember God cares for you and that he said in his Word he would never leave you nor forsake you. So keep pressing in and pressing onward toward the mark.

There were days—let me be honest, weeks—while I was writing this book that I felt like giving up, throwing in the towel. Emotions tried to overtake me with feeling like it was me against the world. People began turning on me, I was in a secluded place, left with nothing but my thoughts. Worried about the people slowly arriving, and quickly departing from my life, and the silence was deafening. I had to hear that if God be for me then that is all that matters. To understand this is my breeding ground for supernatural opportunities and for God to complete a work that he had already begun in me.

For me this has been a time of inward reflection, seeing where God has brought me and then recounting the things that I have learned along the way. I had to be taught patience and that waiting on God's time versus man is something all together different. As man we begin to expect things to happen in our timing, which is for the most part sooner than normal. But when it does not, we still have to hold on and just be still and know that God is still God and his timing is perfect. I also learned that I am never without him, no matter what it looked like in the natural God has never left me or forsaken me. In the natural it may have seemed as if nothing was happening but in the spirit he is ever present and working things out for our good. Most importantly I learned the lesson of trusting him wholeheartedly. That if he said it I can honestly rest assured that it will come to pass.

I am thankful that he allowed me to be the messenger he used to get this message out to the masses. God loves us so much that he does not want to leave us the way he found us but instead clean us up and give us divine purpose. I began crying the other day at the mere thought of completing the task that was given to me. How during this whole process he first had to separate me from the known and bring me to a place that was unknown and unfamiliar to me. In doing so I had to place all my trust and faith in him totally and completely. Now it has become like second nature when it seems as if the bottom is falling out beneath me, I know that I have to give it to God. During this time of writing, he gave me "radical praise." I thought, *Okay, I will praise you even in the midst of the hardships, when people cannot understand how I still have a "yet praise" in my mouth.* Little did they know my faith grew through each trial and tribulation. I began to wait in expectancy for my breakthrough. Knowing that I can thank God in advance when all hopes seems lost has become engraved in my being.

The same is true for you because God is not a respecter of persons; what he can do for others he can and will do for you if you are obedient and allow his will to have reign in your life and die to your flesh daily. God loves you, and he wants to walk with you and bless you so that you can be a blessing to others with your testimony of tenacity and faith. It is time out for games and it is time for a revival to sweep across our great nation and get back to basics, to believe God for your outcome and be the Christian he has called you to be in this day and time. God bless you, and I love you all.

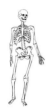

endnotes

1   "Obama more threats" by Eileen Sullivan, Associated Press Writer.

2   Wikipedia online dictionary defines the term "slut."

3   Nelson's NKJV Study Bible for references on submitting Ephesians 5:22–24.

4   Wikipedia online dictionary defines the term "emotional affair."

5   Merriam-Webster online dictionary defines the term "accountability."

6   Encarta World English Dictionary defines the term "bland."

7   "Was U.S. Christian Slain in Muslim Mauritania 'Asking for It'?" By CP Guest Contributor Aaron D. Taylor published on Monday, July 13, 2009 by the *Christian Post*.

8   The new Strong's Complete Dictionary of Bible Words for the term "Christian."

9   Bible.com defines the term "fornication."

10 Wikipedia online dictionary defines the term "pornography."

11 Forbes.com data on what the pornographic industry grosses.

12 Safefamilies.org Statistics on Pornography, Sexual Addiction and Online Perpetrators.

13 Mondofacto dictionary defining "lust."

14 "The Seduction of Pornography and the Integrity of Christian Marriage, An Address" by R. Albert Mohler, Jr., president the Southern Baptist Theological Seminary delivered to the men of Boyce College, March 13, 2004.

15 Wikipedia online dictionary defines the term "polymorphous perversity."

16 Safefamilies.org Statistics on Pornography, Sexual Addiction and Online Perpetrators.

17 The new Strong's Complete Dictionary of Bible Words defines the term "abomination."

18 Encarta World English Dictionary defines the term "abomination."

19 "Why AIDS is becoming a Black woman's disease and what we can do about it"—*Health* by Nikitta Foston Ebony Nov 2002.

20 "Black Women in US 23 Times as Likely to Get AIDS Virus" by Gary Younge published on Tuesday, April 6, 2004 by *The Guardian*/UK.

21 Webster's dictionary defines the term "praise."